Prayers for One Voice

Prayers *for* *One* *Voice*

180 Prayers Based on the Revised Common Lectionary

Everett Tilson
Phyllis Cole

Abingdon Press
Nashville

PRAYERS FOR ONE VOICE: 180 PRAYERS BASED ON
THE REVISED COMMON LECTIONARY

Prayers copyright © 1989, 1990, and 1991 by Abingdon Press
Compilation and Introduction copyright © 1993 by Abingdon Press.

93 94 95 96 97 98 99 00 01 02   —   10 9 8 7 6 5 4 3 2 1

This book is printed on recycled, acid-free paper.

Library of Congress Cataloging-in-Publication Data

Tilson, Everett.
　　Prayers for one voice : 180 prayers based on the revised Common lectionary /
Everett Tilson, Phyllis Cole.
　　　　p.　　cm.
　　Includes index.
　　ISBN 0-687-30339-7 (alk. paper)
　　　　1. Church year—Prayer-books and devotions—English. 2. Occasional services.
I. Cole, Phyllis, 1962–　　. II. Cole, Phyllis, 1962–　　Litanies and other prayers
for the revised Common lectionary.　III. Title.
BV30.T557　　1993
264'.13—dc20　　　　　　　　　　　　　　　　　　　92-42141
　　　　　　　　　　　　　　　　　　　　　　　　　　　　CIP

Except for brief paraphrases, or unless otherwise noted, scripture quotations are from the
Revised Standard Version of the Bible, copyright 1946, 1952, 1971 by the Division of
Christian Education of the National Council of Churches of Christ in the USA. Used by
permission.

MANUFACTURED IN THE UNITED STATES OF AMERICA

To "Group"—
Mike, Pat, Sue, and Paul—
thanks for cradling my heart.

—p. c.

and

To four friends,
Wilson Boots, C. T. Vivian, William Walzer, and Wilson Welch,
whose commitment inspired my unfailing trust
and
never in vain.

—e. t.

Contents

Introduction

Prayers for One Voice is designed to be used in any one of three ways. It may be used as a resource for developing a prayer in worship services organized around the readings for the entire three-year cycle of the revised common lectionary. Or it may be used, following the leads offered in the subject index, to compose a prayer for worship in a less formal setting or service. And since many of these prayers were consciously designed to include all the typical elements of the traditional pastoral prayer—adoration, thanksgiving, confession, repentance, intercession, and petition—it may also be used as an aid in constructing a prayer embodying only one of these elements. For this usage, since the index will be of little help, you will have no alternative to screening the prayers individually.

This volume brings together all the "prayers for one voice" in *Litanies and Other Prayers for the Revised Common Lectionary: Years A, B, and C*. Earlier editions of these three volumes for the unrevised common lectionary appeared in successive years from 1989 to 1991. Not surprisingly, the revision of the lectionary forced us to make changes in some of these prayers. Yet they are not nearly as numerous as the changes in the lections themselves. In many instances the similarities between the old lections and the new were so great that they obviated the need for any adjustments in thought or language.

This resource assumes an intimate connection not only between the Bible and prayer, but also between prayer and vocation. Indeed, prayer may be conceived as a bridge between the Bible and vocation, with traffic moving in both directions. For just as we have drawn on the biblical witness to find appropriate images for the prayers in this volume, we have so elaborated these images as to amplify the tasks to which God calls us in the world.

Before leaving you to your own initiative in the use of this volume, we would urge you to recognize the importance of clothing ideas in appealing language. The current stress in biblical studies on the use of imagery can be traced to this recognition. But imagery, to be clarifying and persuasive, must not only be vivid; it must also be visual. The hearer must be able to see what the speaker says. For this to happen, speakers must put themselves in the position of hearers, just as hearers must put themselves in the position of speakers. We have consciously striven, therefore, for language that will enable the users of this volume to hear with their eyes.

In addition, we would ask you to do one other thing: Alter these prayers in any way that will make them more fully your own—by changing the language for addressing deity, by deleting or substituting paragraphs, by localizing the points of reference. For while we are responsible for the form the prayers take in this book, you are responsible for the form they will take in your worship.

Everett Tilson
Phyllis Cole

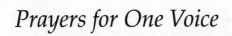

Prayers for One Voice

Year A

Gracious God,

You have spoken to us from the heights. On Mt. Sinai you declared your law and entered into covenant with your people. On Mt. Zion your spirit filled the temple and received the praises of your people. On the Mt. of Olives your Messiah turned aside to pray and began to offer himself as a sacrifice for your people.

We thank you, O God, that, despite being so different from us, you do not ask to be left alone. Instead, you call us to take our place on the mountain. You summon us there to receive your judgment and your peace. And you promise that there we shall behold the One who reveals your glory. Yet while our hearts long to climb your holy mountain, our lives trap us in the valley. We feel helpless to reach our destination. You command us to love our neighbors as ourselves, but we afflict them with cold hearts, quick tempers, thoughtless tongues, and heartless deeds. You call us to become your peacemakers among the nations, but we continue to beat plowshares into warships and pruning hooks into missile heads. For this preoccupation with ourselves and the mischief to which it leads us, we are truly sorry, and we pray for deliverance.

O God, make us open to the people around us and the miserable world in which they live. Multitudes of your children suffer out of sight. Give us open eyes. Today their cries for help are muffled. Give us open ears. Their pain is often borne alone. Give us open hearts. Their hope and healing are ours to grant. Give us open hands.

You tell us, dear Lord, that we owe no one anything except our love. Now we ask you to teach us the cost of that love. Enable us, as you enabled Jesus, to pay that cost in gracious service to humanity. *Amen.*

🍁 *First Sunday of Advent*

Advent Season

❀ *Second Sunday of Advent.* God of the ages, of yesterday, today, and forever, draw near to us. Draw us near to you.

You have promised that you will never stretch out your arm to keep us from your presence. You have said that you will never deny us if our skin is a shade this side of another; you fashioned us in your image. You have said you will never deny us if we call you a name new to another's ears; you knit us together in our mothers' wombs. You have said you will never deny us if one of us is woman and another, man; you created us female and male. You have said you will never deny us if our bodies sometimes fail us where they do not fail another; you did not close your eyes to our frames. You have said you will never deny us if our years are greater than a brother's, or fewer than a sister's; you have known our days since before we were born. You have said you will never deny us if our homes lie in a place distant from this one; you have said that all the nations shall seek you.

These are your promises, Lord. And these are your commandments. You have commanded us to prepare for your kingdom; you have faith in us to make preparations. We shall not be dismayed. We shall sing of your righteousness and do your justice among all men and women and children, whoever and wherever they are. In these people, whose sandals we are not worthy to carry, walks the world's Christ. You have spoken the Word who dwells among us. May we be faithful to the Word you have sent.

❀ *Third Sunday of Advent.* How strong your voice, God! How it thunders across the lands, calling forth blossoms from parched earth and turning back waters from flooded ground. You stand at the world's door and knock; who can withstand the sound of your voice?

How soft your voice, God! How it murmurs in the morning, calling life forth from its bed and hastening the night to its own. You come to us, walking in the garden in the cool of the day; who can hide from the sound of your voice?

Tarry with us, O God. Let your Word love our eyes into seeing again the wounds we inflict on our neighbors. Tarry with us, O God. Let your Word love our ears into hearing again the sounds of a crying creation. Tarry with us, O God. Let your Word love our hands into healing again with the gifts you have granted your children.

If you send us to the wilderness, let our voice join with yours to call forth joy. If you send us to the raging rivers, let our voice join with yours to call forth peace. If you send us to the rulers, let our voice join with yours to call forth humility. Where you send us, we will follow. Our feet shall lift in quiet step to the ends of the earth, for the salvation of our God is come.

✤ *Fourth Sunday of Advent.*   God of heaven and of earth, your sign appears to a faint-hearted people. Your presence makes us tremble; your promise makes us timid.

Soon the veil between earth and sky will be lifted. We have been given a demanding part to play. Our lines are not many. Our movements will be few. But we who are so addicted to activity have been given the cue to wait. We who are so anxious to get ahead have been directed to prepare the way for someone else. We who dream of mansions have been sent to find a manger. We who would be great must kneel before a baby. "Be not afraid"—the angel's words to Mary, to us. But having faith is not being unafraid. Having faith is waiting and preparing and searching and kneeling despite our fear of the unknown; it is having hope despite the odds against us.

Forgive us our faint spirits. Forgive us our timid souls. As we open our arms to the Christ child, clasp us to your breast. Teach us with a firm hand how to refuse the evil and choose the good, and lift us up with a gentle hand when we stumble and fall.

Christmas Season

❀ *Christmas Eve or Day.* Mighty God, rain your power on your people. In a weakened world our hands grow weary, our hearts grow hard. But on this day Great Power is born, not where life is safe, but where life is sorry; not where life is sterile, but where life is soiled; not where life comes easy, but where life is fought for. A baby is born, and the baby lives. Joy to the world; let earth receive her Power!

Wonderful Counselor, send us your Word. In a crying world our speech fades from our lips, our ears close to understanding. But on this day the Word is born, not to endure silence, but to testify to truth; not to muffle our hearing, but to unstop our ears; not to condemn creation, but to transform it. A baby is born, and the baby lives. Joy to the world; let earth receive her Word!

Everlasting Father of hope, Eternal Mother of faith, lend us your joy. In an anxious world our hearts tremble at the thought of tomorrow, our eyes are cast upon the ground. But on this day All Joy is born, not that hearts may yield to gloom, but that they might prepare him room; not that eyes may be bound to earth, but that they might see the glory of heaven. Swaddle our world in your arms, even as the Child was swaddled by Joseph and Mary. A baby is born, and the baby lives. Joy to the world; All Joy is come!

Prince of Peace, grant us *your* peace. In our wounded world our spirits bow to sin, our souls are enslaved by sorrow. But on this day Almighty Peace is born, so that our spirits may not worship other gods, but the God whose rod falls upon the oppressors; so that our souls may not break beneath their burdens but grow strong while carrying the loads of the friendless. A baby is born, and a baby lives. Let heaven and nature sing; let earth receive her Peace!

❀ *First Sunday After Christmas.* Mighty Creator, we marvel at the works of your hands; they never cease to fill us with excitement and wonder. Glorious Redeemer, we thrill to your displays of patience; they kindle within us hope and confidence. Gracious Sustainer, we bow in awe before your unwavering support; even though we constantly let you down, you never fail to hold us up.

For all these mighty works we praise your name, O God. But we thank you most of all for the revelation of yourself in the One whose resting-places were, first, a manger, and, finally, a cross. In him you brought low the proud and raised up the humble. In him you became truly human in order that we, through him, might become truly human.

He taught us well, yet our living has not always made the world more human. Our sympathies, unlike his, do not strengthen the weak. Our words, unlike his, do not condemn the proud. And our deeds, unlike his, do not honor the claims of justice.

We have not become a mirror of him as he became a mirror of you. For this betrayal—of him, of you, and of ourselves—we come before you with contrite hearts. Forgive us, O God, and renew us, that the humanity that was born in Jesus might be reborn in us today.

Today, as when you joined the human race in Jesus, multitudes sit in darkness and walk in the shadow of death. Millions are starving for want of food. Others are hungry for the bread of life. We pray, O Lord, that you will make us the channels of your blessing to the nations, whether they need the bread of earth or the bread of heaven.

Christ has come to bring peace on earth and goodwill to all its peoples. Let us proclaim this Good News, today and tomorrow and forever, here and there and everywhere.

❧ *Second Sunday After Christmas.* Fashioner of things seen and unseen, your hand laid the foundation of the world and peopled the earth with creatures made in your own image. For the beneficence of your creation, and for the magnificence of the universe you are still creating, we offer you praise; we offer you glory.

You have entrusted us with the care of your creative work, and through the centuries you have hoped for leaders worthy of your trust and ours: leaders who would respect creation and its creatures; who would beat swords into plowshares, turn spears into pruning hooks, and do war no more with nature or creature; who would hunger and thirst for wisdom and long for the full coming of your realm on earth. We thank you, O God, that in the fullness of time your search bore fruit. At long last, there appeared among us just such a one—a leader after your own heart and ours. In this One you gave us a foundation on which we could build a new world and a new life.

But we must confess that we have neither loved nor served you as that One did. We have not persevered in the tasks to which that One called us. We have not led earth's refugees to you in their quest for peace, freedom, happiness, and dignity. Thus, they have become strangers to us. We have left them to go their way as if we bear no responsibility for them.

O God, enlighten the eyes of our hearts, that we might wholeheartedly embrace the tasks to which your Chosen One summoned us. Let us go among earth's wanderers; let us see our hidden ones and comfort them, even as we would be comforted. Let us see our disguised ones and accept them, even as we would be accepted. Let us see our despised ones and love them, even as we would be loved. O Lover of the universe, help us to remember our brothers and sisters, even as you remember us.

Guardian of memories and of hopes, you look forward with us to the day when all the world shall rest upon the sure foundation you have laid for it in Jesus Christ. Help us realize the greatness of your power resting within us. You have given us that power, not that our will but that *your* will may be done. As it is in heaven, let us see it done on earth. And when the universe bends its knee before your throne, on that day all the peoples of the earth shall be called by the name that is above every name, the Lord our God, Maker of heaven and earth. O God, make us worthy of that name, and of the spirit of the One you sent to lead us.

Season After Epiphany

❊ *First Sunday After Epiphany (Baptism of the Lord).*
From the beginning, O God, your spirit has moved over the face of the waters. From water, life comes; by water, life is sustained; through water, new life begins.

Help us remember our baptism, O God.

Through your prophet you have told us, "Fear not, for I have redeemed you. I have called you by name, you are mine. When you pass through the waters, I will be with you; when you pass through the rivers, they shall not overwhelm you. You are precious in my eyes, and I love you."

As you fulfill your promise, O God, let us fulfill our baptism. May we hear that still small voice within us saying, "This is my beloved daughter, this my beloved son; with them I am well pleased." Bear patiently our failures to love others as you love them. It is not easy to love. Sometimes we are too proud, sometimes too cold, sometimes too tired, sometimes too hurt to love.

But you, O God, can teach us to love more fully in the spirit of our baptism. Through the spirit we give our lives to your mystery. Renew our faith. Through the spirit we are made members of your body. Renew our unity. Through the spirit we are made aware of our gifts. Renew our ministry.

When we were children, we spoke like children, we thought like children, we reasoned like children. But since our rebirth, we have grown in the faith. Show us how far we have come; and light the lantern that will show us how far we have yet to go.

❊ *Second Sunday After Epiphany.*   O God of Jesus, on whom the Spirit descended and in whom the Spirit lived, we draw near to you in his name. Gathered here in the knowledge that you walked among us in him, we take comfort from your nearness. You are still our Judge, but now we are assured that your judgment will be tempered with justice and your justice, with mercy.

We thank you, gracious God, for the Spirit that dwelled in Jesus. Let that same Spirit descend upon us that we might exclaim with John, "Behold, the Lamb of God!"

O Lamb of God, who takes away the sin of the world, take away our sin. We have seen your mercy, but we resist your call to become its bearers. We have heard your summons to self-giving service, but we still heed the call to self-seeking life. We have tasted the fruit of self-sacrifice, but we continue to relish the fruit of self-indulgence. Deliver us, dear Lord, from our double-mindedness. Help us with purity of heart to serve you with singleness of purpose.

It was too light a thing, O Lord, for your Servant simply to raise up the tribes of Jacob. You sent him, instead, as a light to the nations that your salvation might reach to the ends of the earth. He came to his own people, and they turned their backs to the light. He went to the nations, and they covered their eyes. He came to us, and we shielded our sight. But to as many as received the light, he gave the power to become its bearers.

No matter in which direction we look, O God, we see your people walking in darkness: heeding the call to arms as if the Prince of Peace had never been born, pursuing the cry of mammon as if Jesus had never been crucified for thirty pieces of silver, oppressing our neighbors as if God had never told us to love them as ourselves.

Open our eyes, O Lord, and let the light that shone in Jesus shine in us and through us. And let the light fall also upon our neighbors, that we might become one in our witness to that which dwells in every person ever born on earth.

🍁 *Third Sunday After Epiphany.*   Great Comforter, you wrap your arms around us when we fall and help us stand again. Humble our foolish pride that we may reveal to you our weakness, that you might make us strong; humble us that we may admit our greediness, that you might make us generous; humble us that we may show you our heartlessness, that you might make us merciful.

The temptation to betray you is great. Your ways are not the world's ways. We are tempted to be greater than we should, to be less than we could. We abuse our spirits and our bodies, and we are not content until we also injure the spirits and bodies of your other children. It is not only what we *do* that makes us guilty; it is what we do *not* do.

Walking through the scenes of our daily work and play, Jesus Christ says to us, "Follow me, and I will make you fishers of women and men." Can we, like Peter and Andrew, leave our nets? Not once, but always? Can we, like Mary and Martha, learn the time when we are to wait, and when we are to serve? Can we lay our livelihood, our homes, our way of life on your altar? Or shall we say instead to the Savior, "I must save something back"?

Help us to trust you. We do not know you well. Help us to follow you. We do not know where you lead. Help us to see you. We do not know how to believe. Help us to be your children, O God, for your difficult way sends us scrambling for calves of gold.

Help us, Comforter, for the kingdom, the power, and the glory are yours forever.

❋ *Fourth Sunday After Epiphany.* O God, who tore Israel from the chains of Egypt and delivered the church from the tomb of Calvary, your greatness astounds us. We search the heavens above, and we are overwhelmed by their brilliance. We look at the earth below, and we are mystified by its people. Like the wise men of old, we have traveled far, seeking an explanation of our wonder and confusion. We pray that we have not made this journey in vain. Reward us as you rewarded the sages from the East. Lead us to the manger, that you might enlighten us as you enlightened them.

We have traveled as far to flee from Bethlehem as the wise men journeyed to reach it. They sought Christ among the rich, but they found him among the poor. They sought Christ among the powerful, but they found him among the weak. They sought Christ among the wise, but they found him among the foolish. Yet so often we continue to seek him where they could not find him. Forgive us, O God, for following the world's map to find your treasure.

We have betrayed your gospel by substituting the power of the throne for the power of the cross. And the whole earth shouts the news of our failure. The mighty have grown more corrupt, the crafty have become more devious, and the weak continue to be oppressed. For the sake of these and all your other children, O Lord, let us rediscover the connection between the manger and the cross. Let us not accept the fiction that we can be born of God without first dying to self.

Christ offers us a new understanding of greatness, a different idea of goodness, and a deepened sense of responsibility for our neighbor. He is our wisdom, our righteousness, our sanctification, and our redemption. Therefore, if we must boast, let us boast only in him who glorified the manger and redeemed the cross.

❋ *Fifth Sunday After Epiphany.* Gracious God, we thank you for the light that shone in Jesus, revealing unto us the distance between your goodness and ours. We deplore this gap, yet we rejoice that you chased the darkness that kept it hidden from our eyes. By your light we are both encouraged and condemned. We are reassured to see your face turned in our direction, bidding us to come unto you. But we shudder at the sight of us turning our backs on you, resisting the light that could mirror your glory. We thank you, O God, for leaving your light in the world even though we have not always heeded your summons to become the light of the world. Instead of illuminating your character, we have blurred it. You have commanded us to love you with all our being, but we have consigned our love to the pigeonhole of religion. You have commanded us to love our neighbors as ourselves, but we have been too preoccupied with ourselves to find them. You have called us to be peacemakers, yet we have encouraged the arms makers with our fears and our fortunes. You have summoned us to be wall breakers, yet we have supported the wall makers with our silence and our sympathy. We have seen the light, but we have refused to walk in it.

Yet we long, O Lord, to keep your law and do your will. We ask forgiveness for our rebellion, not merely for the sake of the joy we have denied ourselves, but also for the joy we have denied others. Keep ever before us the needs of the world into which you sent Jesus and for whose sake he gave himself to the uttermost. Let us feel its pain as our own, seek its good as our own, and work for its transformation in the name and spirit of him who came into the world not to condemn but to redeem it.

We listen now, O God, for your word. Let its message illumine our minds that we may will as Jesus willed. Let its spirit quicken our hearts that we may love as Jesus loved. Let its power speed our steps that we may do as Jesus did.

❧ *Sixth Sunday After Epiphany.*   O Lord, you both judge and pardon. In long days past you declared your law among us. Yet, through the centuries of our history and the years of our lives, we have smashed your tablets upon the stones. We have broken your commandments. We cried that your way was too difficult.

So you sent your law again. But instead of making your way easier, this time you tried to write it upon our hearts. You sent Jesus of Nazareth, and he went beyond the letter of the law to its spirit. He declared us guilty before we even acted. He made us aware of the battles that rage within us before accusing us of the wars that rage around us. Not only the actions of our hands, but the motives of our hearts, were put on trial, and we were found wanting.

Yet he forgave us. Even those of us who crucified him. He showed us something terribly important about who you are and how you love, and about how you judge. It is not for your sake, but ours, that you convict us and then give us the freedom to try again. Your law of love is impossible to keep, yet we must try; your forgiveness of sin is impossible to believe, yet we must trust.

Help us to trust that you are greater than the most loving human parent. We humans have an end to our patience and a limit to our strength. Our faith wavers, our hope dims, our love stumbles over pride. But you are infinitely patient and strong beyond compare. Your faith and your hope and your love abide, but the greatest of these is love.

We have heard that it was said in ancient times, "You shall not kill, you shall not commit adultery, you shall not steal, you shall not bear false witness." But today we hear again the greatest of all commandments, that we will love the Lord our God and our neighbors as ourselves.

It is not an easy Way. But as you have chosen us, we chose you. Keep us in the Way we must go, O Lord, our Judge and our Redeemer.

✻ *Seventh Sunday After Epiphany.*   O God, our Teacher of all generations, we praise your holy name. You have dealt with us mercifully, refusing to enlighten us beyond our capacity to understand or to judge us beyond our understanding. When we were children, you allowed us to speak and understand and judge as children. But now that the light of the world has come, you spurn our attempt to return to our childish ways. Now that you have shown us what it means to be fully and truly human, you confront us with adult obligations and you judge us by adult standards. We thank you, dear God, for not letting us run away from ourselves.

In Jesus you revealed to us the humanity you had in mind at our creation. We marvel at the sight of such goodness: that does not strike back when struck; that goes two miles when asked to go only one; that does not refuse the beggar or withhold a loan from the borrower; that returns the hate of the enemy with love; that offers up prayers for persecutors; that salutes foreigners as well as neighbors; and that greets the injustice of the unjust with the justice of the just.

We know all the excuses for not judging ourselves by this standard.

We cannot interpret the Bible literally; we dare not compare ourselves with Jesus; we must not confuse the twentieth century with the first. Yes, we know these excuses, and sometimes they are both relevant and valid. But often they are neither. Grant us the honesty, dear Lord, to acknowledge the darkness within that hides your light from above.

As we seek to recover the relevance of the teaching and example of Jesus, it is not alone for ourselves that we pray. We pray also for this strife-torn world, divided by self-seeking religion and rampant nationalism. Hatred and vengeance stalk the earth: They abuse children too young to know that they are being abused; they terrorize ones too innocent to know the folly of returning evil for evil; and they provide excuses for the peddlers of violence. Forbid that we should continue to aggravate the problem; grant us the grace to become part of the solution. If we cannot take Jesus literally, let us not fail to take him seriously.

Distant from you, dear God, our vision grows dim, our hearing grows dull, and our heart grows weak. Bridge the gap between us, that we might, once again, see with our eyes, hear with our ears, and understand with our hearts. Let us leave this service, renewed and determined, ready both to obey and reveal your holy and righteous will.

❧ *Eighth Sunday After Epiphany.* Gracious God, our Ruler and our Judge, we live in a world of many rulers and judges. But, unlike you, they do not rule with mercy and righteousness. Unlike you, they do not judge with justice for the weak and equity for the meek. We give thanks, O God, that you are above them all.

In Christ you have taught us to bow before no ruler but you and to fear no judgment but yours. Yet we daily betray that teaching. We seek the applause of those who do not honor you. We praise the decisions of those who rule without your mercy. And we court the approval of those who oppress the weak.

Forgive us, dear Lord, for using heaven's name to seek earth's rewards. Cleanse our hearts of their fickle habits and enable us to spurn earth's rewards for heaven's sake.

Multitudes of your children throughout the earth make no claim to have found the way, to have seen the light, or to have discovered the truth. Unlike them, we *do* make that claim, in the name of Jesus Christ. Yet all too many of your children have not been brought nearer to you by our example. Many who have turned to us in search of you have turned away from you because of us. So we pray, O Lord, for the renewal in us of the vision with which Jesus enlightened us. As servants of Christ and stewards of your mysteries, lead us to reflect the light and reveal the truth. Empower us, as you empowered him, to hail our acceptance of you, even if it means our rejection by the world.

We ask, dear Lord, that today's worship will strengthen us for tomorrow's task. Grant us clarity of mind that we may see you clearly; purity of heart, that we may love you truly; and steadfastness of purpose, that we may serve you faithfully.

❧ *Last Sunday After Epiphany (Transfiguration Sunday).*

O God, you call us up from the valleys to your mountain. Your mountain was not made by human hands but fashioned by your fingers. It has not stood against the floods for a day, or a year, but since a time lost to human memory. It is your dwelling place, your throne, your footstool. How amazed we are to know that with such a home you do not choose to remain distant from us. Just as you call us up, you rush down to meet us. Thank you for filling our valleys and making them plains.

You called your Son to carry on this work. You sent him to save us from the pitfalls we did not see and to deliver us from those we carved for ourselves. Now, as your sons and daughters, we are called to do the same. But we are afraid. Though your hand of mercy touches us, we are afraid to touch our own lives, much less the lives of strangers. We are reluctant to change life where it is familiar and comfortable, even when we know we should and how we could.

We pray for ourselves and for others of your frightened children. Lift up our eyes. Help us to see where we can begin making changes. If someone requires our time, help us to give it. If someone asks for our patience, help us to grant it. If someone cries for understanding, help us to find it. If someone argues for a different way, help us to examine it. If someone needs a generous hand, help us to offer it. If someone wants to bless our lives, help us to receive it. If someone struggles beneath a burden, help us to carry it. If someone suffers from a wrong we have done, help us to mend it.

O Lord, hear our prayer. Your way is so easy when we are standing on the mountaintop. There, at a distance from the rest of the world, we feel forgiven, loved, reassured. We are so tempted to remain with you. But you send us with your blessing and your mission back to those places from which we came. Be our vision, O God! Help us to see!

Lenten Season

❦ *First Sunday in Lent.* O God, who gave the heavens their glory and the earth its beauty, we marvel at the grandeur of your universe. It bears eloquent witness to the distance between Creator and creature. Yet you narrowed that distance by creating us in your own image and making us stewards of your creation. We thank you not only for the glory of the world in which you have placed us, but for the responsibility you have bestowed on us for its care.

Just as we marvel at the splendor of your creation, you must marvel at the shallowness of your creatures. With us, as with our first parents, you have been generous to a fault. You have given us a land rich in harvest. You have given us a culture steeped in learning. You have given us an economy famous for its technology. You have given us a political system envied for its democratic traditions. We thank you, dear God, for having blessed us with so vast a treasure. And we thank you, too, for permitting us to reap where we did not sow and to build on foundations laid by others.

As we recall these gifts that we so greatly enjoy but for which we did not labor, we are moved to humble confession. Not only have we failed to pay our ancestors their dues, we have not given you yours. We have sometimes treated these gifts as if *we* were their creators. We have often forgotten that without you we would have none of them. Then, when we did remember that you were their source, we neglected to recall the purpose for which you gave them.

You gave us an abundant harvest to feed the hungry, but people still die of starvation. You gave us an advanced culture to spread the joy of learning, but people still wallow in ignorance. You gave us technology to enhance the quality of life, but people are still living in misery. You gave us democracy to model the virtues of freedom, but people still doubt our practice of the freedom we proclaim. So we ask forgiveness for our failure of memory and courage.

Refresh our memory and renew our courage, O God, that we might reveal the source of our gifts by the way we use them. Let us dedicate our harvest to the war on starvation; our learning, to the war on ignorance; our technology, to the war on misery; and our democracy, to the war on oppression. Let us intercede for these victims of injustice, if we dare. But let us never forget that you expect us to intercede with our deeds as well as with our words.

O Lord, though rich, for our sake, you became poor. Teach us so to invest our gifts that, through us, your kingdom may come on earth as in heaven.

❧ *Second Sunday in Lent.*   O God who lies beyond us, O Friend who dwells within us, hear our prayer. You are the source of life; in you we are born. But your word announces that we must be born again. That word confuses us.

Nicodemus, a man well versed in your scriptures and gifted as a teacher, could not understand what it meant. Bewildered, he could slip away and find Jesus, even if he had to go under the cover of night; he could debate it with your Son. To whom are we to turn? Can anyone tell us the answer?

Perhaps no answer can be simply spoken. Nicodemus left Jesus, frowning as deeply as when he had come. Later he was a member of the body that condemned Jesus and delivered him to Pilate. But after Jesus had been crucified, Nicodemus risked his life to help Joseph of Arimathea bury him. Perhaps even then he did not understand; yet, even at that very moment, he may have been working out his faith, despite his lack of understanding. Despite his lack of answers.

We must be born again. The word confuses us. But keep our confusion from standing as a stumbling block. You do not ask that we arrive at correct beliefs; you call us to journey through acts of faith. You do not judge our minds for falling short in their understanding of you and your ways; you judge our hearts for growing hard in their loyalty to us and *our* ways. And your forgiveness enables us to struggle back to our feet, take a deep breath, and begin walking again.

We celebrate you, Comforting One, for understanding us better than we understand ourselves. You planned well. You knew a physical birth would not be enough; you knew we could not see you with the eyes of flesh. You called us then and you call us now to another birth. Help us see you with the eyes of faith.

❧ *Third Sunday in Lent.*   Lord of the harvest, your rains fall upon the evil and the good; your winds caress the wicked and the righteous; your sun warms the vile and the virtuous. Your seeds are scattered with the breeze; your sowing does not scorn any soil.

In our more honest moments, we number ourselves among the good, the righteous, and the virtuous. And, in our *more* honest moments, we claim to be more deserving of your care than the evil, the wicked, and the vile. We contend that we have worked harder, sacrificed more, and earned a greater share of your love.

Humble our pride, Lord. Your love is greater than human love. You do not love only those who love you. You love your enemies and do good to those who hate you; you bless those who curse you and understand those who abuse you. You lend, expecting nothing in return; you are kind to the ungrateful and the selfish.

We have forgotten just how perfect your loving is. And we have forgotten just how prideful our living is. We have forgotten that, while most of us would not sacrifice ourselves even for the godly, Christ died for the ungodly.

Let us remember that you are both Judge and Savior. If you were only our Judge, you would have no choice but to condemn us. Measured by you, which of us could stand without guilt and blame? But you are also our Savior, our Redeemer, our Deliverer, our Hope. Embraced by you, which of us would remain guilty and blameworthy?

Humble our pride, Lord. Convict us, and we will not think more highly of ourselves than we should; console us, and we will accept our humanity; consecrate us, and we will receive our identity as your people.

❦ *Fourth Sunday in Lent.*   Dear God, we come before you, a fearful and confused people. Many shadows haunt the world in which we live. Nation lifts up sword against nation. Governments hail the pursuit of peace at the summit, but down in the valley they continue to manufacture arms. Peoples extol the virtues of tolerance, but they turn their differences into occasions for saber-rattling. If we had to depend on ourselves for strength, we could only despair of the future. And if we had to rely on the light within us for illumination, we would have to reconcile ourselves to the darkness. But thanks to you, O God, we can embrace the future with hope. You have enlightened us with your light, given not only for us but for all the people who inhabit the earth. We thank you for granting us deliverance from our fear and clarity for our confusion.

At our baptism we took a vow to walk in your way. We promised to follow you in our quest for the truth and to reflect your light. Then we were so confident of your love for us that we never doubted we would remain loyal to you. But our allegiance to you has wavered. We have strayed from your way to pursue more exotic paths. We have neglected your truth to chase the less demanding wisdom of the world. We have shunned the light to reap the rewards of the dealers in darkness. But we have not gotten off scot-free. We have sown the wind, and we are reaping the whirlwind. The exotic paths have offered endless variety, only to aggravate our insecurity and anxiety. The truths of the world's wisdom have kept us preoccupied, only to leave us disappointed with the fruit of our labors. And we have pursued earth's rewards, only to discover that they have corrupted us before moth and rust could corrupt them.

Yet we come to you, dear God, in full confidence that you will greet us not only as our judge but also as our friend. So we beseech you for wisdom greater than our wisdom, for vision greater than our vision, and for strength beyond our strength. Befriend us anew, that our enemies may no longer have dominion over us; and that we, by our style of life and integrity of witness, may win friends for you and the gospel.

❧ *Fifth Sunday in Lent.*   Great God, you create life. In our hearts we know this, but we cannot comprehend what it means. You have set us in a world that reaches farther than our vision, that runs deeper than our wisdom, that ranges wider than our understanding. Yet you have entrusted it to our care. We grasp it in our hands and try to refashion it, to see it in a new way, to invent what has never been. But, unlike you, we cannot create something from nothing. We must depend on you, for only you can raise up life where life has never lived.

Great God, you conquer death. In our hearts we know this, but we cannot comprehend what it means. You bring us into a world that frightens us beyond our courage, that weakens us beyond our strength, that stretches us beyond our belief. Yet you have entrusted it to our care. We see it lying there in the palm of our hands, almost wanting to give it back, to let you have your way with it without giving us a say. But it is not ours to return. We must depend on you, for only you can raise up life where life has never lived.

We praise you, O God, and our praises humble us. You call to the tomb and life comes out; so simply you say it, and, behold, it is done. But when we are called to the tomb, sometimes we run to hide. Give us hearts stout with courage that we may not hide from those who suffer. Give us shoulders broad with strength that we may walk with the wounded. Give us spirits quiet with humility that we may call forth new life in your name.

Be with those whose souls and bodies need your soothing touch. You know their needs; return them to us with your power that, through your presence, we might resurrect and restore, revive and renew.

> Where there is hatred, let us sow love; . . .
> Where there is doubt, faith;
> Where there is despair, hope;
> Where there is darkness, light; and
> Where there is sadness, joy.
> *Saint Francis of Assisi*

May we be creators with you in life; may we be conquerors with you in death, in the name of Christ Jesus.

❦ *Passion/Palm Sunday.*

Gracious God, our Savior, we marvel at your presence in Jesus. We like to think that, if we had been there, we would have treated you with the respect you deserved: that we would have found majesty in lowliness, greatness in meekness, strength in nonviolence, truth in service, and glory in sacrifice; that we would have seen with our eyes, heard with our ears, understood with our hearts, and recognized Jesus of Nazareth as the servant of the Lord and the Christ of God; that, instead of a crucifixion, there would have been a coronation; and that the triumphal entry would not have been mocked by Good Friday. But we know that the outcome would have been the same. The only difference would have been the names of the actors.

As we think of the actors who played in this Holy Week drama, we recall their performance with pain and anguish. We have walked in the shoes of each of them. Like Judas, we have put money ahead of loyalty to Christ. Like the disciples in Gethsemane, we have put physical comfort ahead of loyalty to Christ. Like the chief priests, we have put inherited beliefs ahead of loyalty to Christ. Like Peter in the courtyard, we have put self-interest ahead of loyalty to Christ. Like Pontius Pilate, we have put public pressure ahead of loyalty to Christ. And like the soldiers, we have put duty ahead of loyalty to Christ. We have not mocked Christ as they did, by plaiting for him a crown of thorns. We have mocked him, instead, by plaiting for him a crown of roses.

We beg your forgiveness, O God, for our presence in the company of these mockers. Yet we are even more embarrassed by our *absence* from the company of those who have remained loyal to Christ. After Calvary, the betrayers in the Garden died for the sake of their loyalty to Christ. So did Stephen. And Paul. And others have followed in their train—risking honor, fortune, reputation, health, and life itself for the sake of the will and the claim of Jesus Christ. We ask your forgiveness, dear Lord, for our failure to follow in their footsteps. We pray for courage that we might relieve Simon the Cyrenian of the burden of having to bear the cross of Jesus alone.

We pray, O God, that the light that brightened the path to Calvary will illumine our path. Let it not only lead us to do as Jesus did, but let it lead others to join us in making the mission of Jesus their mission. Let us hear our Lord say to them and to us, upon observing our common response to the hungry, the naked, the imprisoned, the sick, the homeless, the aged, and the oppressed, "Truly, I say to you, as you did it to one of the least of these, you did it to me."

We recall, O Lord, the prayer of Jesus to be spared the cup of agony, but he put your will before his prayer. Let us repeat that prayer, if we dare, but let us not refuse the cup of agony if you ask us to drink it.

✤ *Holy Thursday.*   O Christ, you knew the hearts of your disciples at the Last Supper but did not flee from their presence. And you know the hearts of your followers here tonight; still you do not flee. Your mercy astounds us; you welcome us to your table, though we are no more worthy than were those first disciples. Gratefully we take our place in your presence and call upon your name, not because our goodness qualifies us to do so, but because your grace invites us to do so.

We thank you, dear Lord, for the message of the Last Supper. When we read about your washing the disciples' feet, we feel the heavenly presence in your human figure, testifying once and for all to the gospel truth about the God whom we all serve and adore. We see you, the messenger of God, coming among us not as a master demanding special privileges, but as a servant performing menial tasks; not as a ruler impressing your importance upon others, but as a lover proclaiming the importance of others to you; not as a lawgiver saddling us with a new set of rules, but as a lifegiver endowing us with a new source of power; not as a dictator coercing our obedience, but as a motivator strengthening our resolve.

We only wish that our resolve were stronger. But we dare not make such a claim. By thought and word and deed we have betrayed your call to love others as you have loved us. Time and again we have broken bread together, sharing the visible sign of your broken body; yet time and again we have remained blind to other members of your living body. Though we are members of one another, we have often centered our lives on ourselves, acting as though we bear no responsibility for the welfare of all.

For thus seeking to divide the community whose union you blessed with your life and sanctified with your love, we are truly sorry, O Christ, and we ask your forgiveness. Renew our appreciation for and commitment to your entire body, which is creation and all that dwells therein. Inspire us again with a sense of its oneness and its purpose; help us to celebrate with joy the dependence of each of your creatures upon the other.

Wars and rumors of wars will continue to divide us until all the world knows this great and gracious truth. Therefore we pray: Enable us so to live in the household of faith that others will see and exclaim of us, as centuries ago they exclaimed of your followers, "Behold, how they love one another!"

❧ *Good Friday.* Almighty God, Creator of the universe and Lord of all creation, whose power knows no limits but the limits you set for yourself, we adore you. We adore you not only for your matchless power; we adore you, above all, for your matchless love.

O God, we thank you for the love that, in Jesus, emptied itself of deity to share the lot of humanity: for the love that forsook the silk of lofty mansions for the straw of a lowly manger; the love that traded a canticle by a royal choir for the song of simple shepherds; the love that spurned the salute of local rulers for the tribute of foreign sages. This love, so abundantly evident in the events surrounding Christ's birth, was no less evident through all the days of his life. We thank you, dear Lord, that in the love of Christ you revealed not only the love with which you love us, but also the love with which we are to love you and one another.

We must confess that we have often betrayed that love. We have neither loved you with all our hearts nor our neighbor as ourselves. We have been quick to mourn the passion of Christ but slow to mirror his passion for justice; quick to condemn his critics but slow to embrace his causes; quick to sing hymns in praise of his courage but slow to perform deeds in pursuit of his mission.

Gracious Lord, with sorrow we confess that we have thus betrayed the cross of Christ, as well as our own humanity. Renew our faith; restore our resolve, that we may heed Christ's summons to take up our cross. Daily send us forth in his spirit to serve humanity with hearts and hands open to those around us who are so very like the multitudes for whom Jesus took up his own cross. Remove from our eyes the shield that blinds us to those in desperate need: the neglected children whose homes are hovels and whose parents are strangers; the bewildered youths whose friends are dropouts and whose heroes are addicts; the distraught adults whose jobs are gone and whose hopes are dashed; the dejected elderly whose companions have died and whose health is fading. As we behold this multitude, let us do as did our brother Christ: Let us take pity upon them, and let us be relentless in seeking change until there be no more need for pity.

Easter Season

❦ *Easter.* O Lord, how you conquer! Not with a birth in a palace, but with a bed in a manger! Not with a threat to end the world, but with a promise to begin a new age! Not with a blow from your mighty hand, but with a turn of your cheek! Not with an uprising against your enemies, but with the uplifting of your Son on a cross! Not by filling the graves with rivals you have defeated, but by emptying the tomb of the Son you have defended!

O Lord, how you conquer! You sent someone we were not expecting, and we came to love him late. Our eyes had become accustomed to other masters. From the time we were small, we had been taught to make something of ourselves; we were not ready for you to make something of us. We had been taught to defend ourselves; we were not ready to defend someone else. So when you sent your Son, though we wanted to follow, we did not know how. He demanded change. We could not give it. So we gave him up—to die.

We still do. Every day. Turning, hiding, fleeing, denying, we give you up to the world. We can be your disciples in the night while everyone sleeps. But when the sun rises, we closet our faith. We do not want to be different from everybody else, so you are crucified in our place.

Forgive us, Lord. Conquer us as only you can conquer. Love us into submission. Lead us to the empty tomb; let us know you are greater than the greatness of our sin. Then lead us back to our homes, our schools and workplaces, that in the power of your forgiveness we may change. Not for our sake, but for yours. Not for our sake, but for theirs. We will set our spirits on the demands of heaven that we may send our hearts to the defense of earth.

We place the earth in the hands of the One who rolled away the stone. May you touch those who are empty and make them filled; may you touch those who are filled beyond their measure and ease their burden. Touch your world through us, even as you did through Jesus Christ. We offer our lives to you for resurrection. Triumphant Victor, into your hands we commend our spirits!

❦ *Second Sunday of Easter.* God of Peace, God of Glory, your gentle might amazes us. When you have most reason to scorn us, you accept us. When you have greatest reason to spite us, you forgive us. When you have infinite reason to forget us, you remember us.

And you remember us with such compassion. When we have locked ourselves away in the upper rooms of our lives, you have sent your presence into our midst with a word of peace. Not blame, not accusation, not condemnation, but peace. You send us peace so that you can send us out from our hiding places with strength and power. All you ask is that we believe.

Believing does not come easily. A little bit of Thomas doubts within us, testing us as much as we test you. Do we believe that we can do what you ask of us, despite the risks? Do we understand that there *will* be risks? In some places of our world, to believe would be to hazard our very lives. What of here? When you are sending us out, what are you asking us to leave behind? O Lord, are we able? We who have not seen, though we believe, shall we be able to act upon our belief?

God of Peace, God of Glory, on your people pour your power! Comfort us in our doubting and strengthen us in our believing. Help us lay all of our lives at your feet—from our doubt to our certainty, from our weakness to our strength, from our humility to our pride, from our patience to our anxiety, we give you all. Transform it, make our lives new. And despite our fear and trembling, send us. We know that wherever we shall go, you shall go before us.

✤ *Third Sunday of Easter.*   Mighty God, Creator of all life, grant us life! Without you—all earth, all breath, all things new and old, all dreams, all visions, all music made, all stories told—nothing would be. In the twinkling of your eye our world appeared and began to dance the dance of the cosmos. If ever your eye would fail to behold it, it would surely collapse in the rubble of doom.

How grateful we are that your promise is sure, that your love is eternal. You have been with us since the dawn of our days. The name you gave us was written on our hearts before we were born. Yet, even though we are yours, you do not promise that we will never be threatened by life's whirling waters. You vow, instead, that when we pass through those waters you shall be with us. You do not promise that we will not be endangered by life's raging fires. You declare, instead, that when we walk through those flames you shall not desert us. For lo, you are with us always, even to the end of the world.

Why do you care so much? Why do you fight for us amidst flames and floods? Do we dare ask *why?* Your assurance comes through the prophet's words: "Because you are precious in my eyes, and I love you."

We are your witnesses, Lord. Having seen your grace at work, we covet your care. Forgive us in our wayward moments for wanting to hoard your care for ourselves. When we request your mercy, let us request it also for others. When we seek your presence, let us seek it also for others. When we cry for strength, let us cry also for others.

Help us, O God, to live as your children, loving and serving you with all our heart and all our soul and all our might. Then we shall believe and understand and know that you are the One. Before you, no other god ever was, and besides you, no other savior lives. O God of our risen Christ, re-create us, redeem us, resurrect us! You have called us by name. Let us heed your call and return the glory to that Name which is above every name.

❦ *Fourth Sunday of Easter.* The triumphal entry, the Temple's cleansing, the Final Supper, the Garden of Gethsemane, then arrest, betrayal, denial, trial, and death. . . . How brief was his life, how fast was his fall. How faithless his friends, how fateful his foes. And yet we are *his* disciples. *He* is our master and leader, our teacher and friend. We are his sinners, he is our savior. Would that he were saved from us!

His speech was straightforward, yet he was condemned by lies. His intent was to be faithful, yet he was accused of treachery. His life was pure, yet he died a criminal's death.

O God, you command us to follow in his steps. You say his wounds have healed us. O Shepherd and Guardian of our souls, though the way be difficult, we believe! In the spirit of those who looked for you in the empty tomb, we believe! In the spirit of those who stood before you in the upper room, we believe! In the spirit of those who walked with you on the road to Emmaus, we believe! In the spirit of those who broke bread with you that morning by the sea, we believe!

Lend your presence to us now, that we might see your will. We long to follow faithfully. If we do good and our works are applauded, let us accept the praise humbly, mindful of your grace. And if we do good and our works are denounced, let us bear the ridicule patiently, assured of your support. Be our Vision, our Wisdom, and our Guide. You only can we truly trust, who justly judges and surely saves.

❦ *Fifth Sunday of Easter.* Gracious God, in whom we live and move and have our being, we thank you for the relationship that you made possible through Jesus Christ. In him you drew near to us that in him we might draw near to you. When we ponder our ingratitude for your grace, we marvel at your forbearance. We thank you, not only for your loving patience but, even more, for your patient loving.

Before Jesus left his disciples, he promised that they would do greater works than he. In Paul and his colleagues that promise was fulfilled. They traversed unpaved roads and turbulent seas to proclaim the rule of Christ to the far corners of the earth. They were confronted by people who greeted them with suspicion, hostility, and even hatred. Yet they remained faithful in the pursuit of their mission. And, because of them, many believed.

In Thessalonica, they were hailed as people who had turned the world upside down. When we compare their resources for spreading the gospel with ours, we are moved to shame. We are not accused of turning the world upside down. Whereas they did terribly much with terribly little, we have done terribly little with terribly much.

So we pray, O God, for your forgiveness, not only for our timidity and cowardice, but also for our laziness and apathy. Endow us with the passion and compassion, the enthusiasm and devotion, the love and commitment with which you endowed those disciples of yours who turned the world upside down for Jesus Christ.

As we think of what could have been, we can only lament what is. The world could have become one in its labor for the mission Jesus set in motion in Nazareth of Galilee. The hungry would not be going unfed; the homeless, unhoused; the sick and afflicted and imprisoned, unvisited; the naked, unclothed; or the poor, untouched by the gospel of Jesus Christ.

We pray, gracious Lord, for the renewal of our zeal. Turn us inside out that we, like Paul and Silas, might turn the world upside down for you.

❧ *Sixth Sunday of Easter.* O God who feeds the hungry and satisfies the thirsty, we have no need that you cannot meet. Your comfort lifts us up when we are depressed, and your power humbles us when we are proud. Your courage strengthens us when we are afraid, and your peace calms us when we are embattled.

Your faithfulness is no accident. And our faith in you is not born of chance. We test you at every turn. We bargain with you, tempt you, abandon you, blame you. Yet you continue to forgive us. Your patience is a match for your understanding. You understand the pain that drives us to despair—the child who goes another way, the parent who will not let the child grow up; the spouse who separates; the friend who drinks to ruin; the companion who suffers, the partner who dies. Oh, yes, you understand. You know all about betrayal and anger and sorrow and loss.

Take our pain, Lord, and bury it in the tomb. Too long it has been buried deep within us. Bury it in the tomb so that, on a day soon to come, new life shall walk forth from its shadows, new rivers shall flow in the deserts, new fountains shall shoot up in the valleys, and pools of water shall give refreshment in the wilderness.

Then, Lord, we will see and know and understand together: Your hand shall have done this; we will be reborn, and by your hand brought back into the world.

❀ *Seventh Sunday of Easter.*   Gracious God, we come before you in prayer, not because we know how or what to ask, but because we know there is no one else to whom we can turn. We know, too, that you will meet us where we are and as we are, even though we betray the goodness for which we praise you and are quicker to demand justice than to grant it. When we ponder our faithful moments, we bless you for having created us in your image; but when we consider our unfaithful moments, we bless you for not having remade yourself in our image.

Waiting together after Jesus' departure, the disciples were assured the Holy Spirit would empower them to become witnesses for Christ and to continue his works. Sometimes, more conscious of the absence than the presence of the Holy Spirit, we feel no great surge of power charging through us. Not only do we acknowledge our weakness, O God, but we are ready to assume responsibility for it. Many of our tasks hardly require our strength; they certainly do not demand yours. Others, instead of advancing your purpose, frustrate it. Forgive us, dear God, for not using the powers you have given us or, worse, for not enlisting them in the service of your will. Forgive us, too, for complaining about the cost of discipleship or, worse, for confusing inconvenience with sacrifice. Deliver us from the temptation to compound the sin of loose talk with the search for cheap grace.

When things go wrong, we accuse you of hiding your face from us. We associate you only with life's good things—good health, good relationships, good food, good clothes, good housing, and good fortune. Yet things sometimes go badly for us. And we turn against you for having turned against us. We forget our Lord's reminder that in the world we would have tribulation. We also forget the prophets, apostles, martyrs, and saints from whose path we stray by our pursuit of the Primrose Lane to Paradise.

We beg your forgiveness, O God, for our failure of memory and of faith. Teach us the lessons of true discipleship. Help us count and pay the cost without complaint or regret. Let us seek suffering neither for its own sake nor for the sake of human praise. Yet, if we cannot serve Christ without bearing reproach, let us rejoice. Let us remember the true meaning of the cross: that it is not merely the tree on which Jesus died, but the faith by which his disciples live.

Hear our prayer, O Lord, and incline us to seek its answer in obedience to your will.

Season After Pentecost

❧ *Pentecost.* Pentecost . . . the seventh Sunday after Easter. How delighted we are, O God of the world, to discover that the empty tomb was not the final act in your drama. The last curtain didn't come down even after the Emmaus walk. What came down was your Spirit— not swooping down like a dove as before, but rushing like a mighty wind and burning like sweet tongues of fire. And when your Spirit came upon your disciples, you had the final word, eternally spoken. It sounded something like:

"For I so love the world . . ."

Your love amazes us. Unlike human love, it shows no partiality. Your eye watches over the people of all languages and lands; your hand lifts the inhabitants of all countries and colors. Unlike human love, your love is not earned. Your help extends to the sinner and the saint; your voice beckons to the wicked and the good. Unlike human love, your love does not fail to forgive what is condemned. Your face shines on the condemned that their ways might change; your ear hears that their ways might change; your ear hears the whispers of their hearts better than their own.

We would pray that you make us worthy, Lord. But you do not ask the impossible. So, instead, we pray that you would make us wise, that we might see what is possible. Help us to absorb the light that shines in the darkness. Help us to breathe in your Spirit that inspires the weak. Then we shall throw open the shutters and rush from the upper room into the streets. And the whole world shall wonder at our words and our deeds. Some may mutter, others grumble; but some shall see and be glad. They shall hear and rejoice, for they shall know that you are our help.

❧ *Trinity Sunday (First Sunday After Pentecost).* We come before you, O God, with joyful and grateful hearts. We adore you, dear Lord, not primarily for what you have done for us, but for who you are: You, our God, are the Lord of all peoples; you, our Creator, are the Creator of all peoples; you, our Redeemer, are the Redeemer of all peoples; you, our Sustainer, are the Sustainer of all peoples. We thank you, O God, that you have come among us and remain with us, not alone to be our Companion, but to be the Companion of the world.

Yet your friendly move in our direction is not always met by our friendly move in your direction. Often we act as if we were the potter and you the clay; as if, instead of your putting us in debt to you by your self-giving, we were putting you in debt to us by our self-giving; and as if, instead of your empowering us to be your witnesses, we were empowering you to be our witness. We call you Lord, dear God, but we cast ourselves in the role of master and you in the role of servant.

But we end up fooling nobody, not even ourselves. When we make our good our goal, we achieve it only to wish we had not. We are as disappointed with ourselves as you and our neighbors are disappointed with us.

We pray, O Lord, that the unity of the Godhead will deepen our appreciation for the unity of humankind. As you come into the world not to condemn but to redeem it, send us into the world to replace hatred with understanding, oppression with justice, envy with loyalty, despair with hope, and futility with purpose. Bring others to you through us, as through others you have brought us to you, that we might become one even as you are one.

❦ *Sunday Between May 29 and June 4 (if After Trinity Sunday).* Giver of all good gifts, Provider of the Spirit, endow us with your love, that we might love the unlovable, and with your joy, that we might reassure the discouraged. Grant us your peace, that we might soothe the embattled, and your endurance, that we might carry the troubled. Bless us with your gentleness, that we might tame the wild, and with your humility, that we might subdue the proud. Send us your patience, that we might calm the angry, and with your faith, that we might trust the unknown.

Teacher of all truths, Proclaimer of the gospel, give us your Word. Let it convict us in our failings. Shine its light on our souls; conceal none of the corners wherein we might hide. Though we fear the pronouncement of the Word, we realize that its judgment opens the way for justice. Our sin will run from the light, and the sun of your forgiveness will inhabit those hiding places where sin once crouched. And in the power of your forgiveness we will turn our hearts to the right.

Shepherd of all creatures, Parent of the prodigal, welcome us home. If we are lost, hurry to find us. If we hesitate at the gate, pick us up in your arms and carry us in. We stray from the paths on which you lead and are trapped on the side of steep cliffs; lift us to safety. We stray from our own sense of right and wrong and become ensnared in the clutches of the world; bring us back to your door.

Architect of all worlds, Planner of the universe, place us firmly on the foundation you laid with your Son as the cornerstone. Mold us, shape us into your living temple. Build your hope on us for future generations. Help us intuit the trust you invest in us, the spirit with which you inspire us, the joy with which you bring us into being.

> Endow us with your gifts, O God.
> Teach us your truths, O Lord.
> Bring us home, O Savior.
> Make us your people, O Creator of all.

❧ *Sunday Between June 5 and June 11 (if After Trinity Sunday).* O Great Physician, you have made it known that those who are well have no need of your healing touch. But how well do we understand what you mean? You sent your Son to the sinners, *for* the sinners. Do we understand fully that we are among their number?

How our pride is offended! You do not save us because of the saintliness of our characters, the worthiness of our spirits, or the splendidness of our reputations. You save us—despite all the good deeds we do and regular tithes we give and faithful prayers we say—because we cannot save ourselves. All your creatures fall short of salvation without your saving hand.

Salvation. A strange word for some of us. Resurrection. Rebirth. Rescue, renewal, revival of our spirits by your Spirit. How vulnerable you ask us to become! Do we know how to let go, to let you fill us, guide us, comfort us, love us? We do not so easily let others into our lives, even those whom we know and adore. How, then, shall we overcome our skeptical doubt and cynical fear to let the unknown enter in?

Break through our self-protecting walls, O Spirit of power! Some of the walls have been erected by our anger, some by sorrow, some by despair; others have been built by envy, some by greed, some by simple fear. Come to us as the parent comes to the child, with forgiving and reassuring arms. If we refuse you from without, persistently call us from within.

Help us to know, Healer of hearts, the truth about ourselves. Help us to return to you and acknowledge our shortcomings. In our distress we seek your face. Finding you, we will behold ourselves clearly in the mirror you hold before us. Then we will take heart and change with you what must be changed, and we will praise with you what is worthy of praise.

❧ *Sunday Between June 12 and June 18 (if After Trinity Sunday).* O God of grace abounding and love unlimited, we thank you for your infinite mercy. It has been the source of our life and faith through all our days, and before that, through the days of our ancestors. When the whip of Pharaoh held Israel in bondage, you broke the yoke of the tyrant, and the prisoners escaped. When the exiles in Babylon trembled before their captors, you raised up a deliverer, and the refugees returned. And when their descendants believed their sin had doomed them to life without hope, you sent your Son, and the hopeless rejoiced. Not only did you redeem them from their sin, but you reconciled them in the midst of their sin. We thank you, dear Lord, that where sin abounds, grace much more abounds.

You call us to be a priestly people and a holy nation, but we, like lost sheep, go astray. We know that peace comes through openness to our neighbors, but we make little effort to crash the walls between us. We know that the soft answer turns away wrath, but we greet our enemies with hard words and even harder looks. We know that self-giving breeds self-givers, but we refuse others the grace with which you treat us. We criticize fellow believers for not patterning their lives after Jesus, yet we do not mirror his life. Forgive us, O God, for our betrayal of your call. Let us take our place at the foot of the mountain of revelation. Open our ears that we might hear your commandments, and transform our hearts that we might keep your covenant. Let us now, as when we first believed, exclaim, "All that the Lord has spoken we will do, and we will be obedient."

As we think of your other sheep who have gone astray, we think of ourselves as your instruments for bringing them home. If they tarry for a sympathizing tear, let us shed it without shame. If they wait for a soothing word, let us speak it without hesitation. If they desire a cup of water, let us offer it without delay. If they hunger for a decent meal, let us provide it without suspicion. Remembering that you are not impressed by gracious words unaccompanied by generous deeds, make us the instruments of your grace in speech and in action.

We are your people, O God; grant us the wisdom to affirm your claim upon us. We await your revealing word; grant us the sensitivity to hear your demands in clear and compelling language. We long to do your will on earth as in heaven, our Heavenly Parent; grant us the courage to fail neither you nor your children.

❧ *Sunday Between June 19 and June 25 (if After Trinity Sunday).* O God, you possess all beginnings and all endings. In the morning you are the cradle of the world and in the evening you are the world's comforter. You are the morning dew kissing the buds of the flowers and the evening mist rising through the falling leaves. You are the early sun announcing the dawning of a new day and the twilight whispering the secrets of another.

You possess all beginnings and endings, all fallings and risings, all living and dying. All of your people, all of your creation swells with the rhythms of life and death and rebirth. These rhythms compel us to sing, to laugh, to dance, to dream. We sing of sorrows borne despite anguish and of joys known despite fear. We laugh at mistakes made in our weakness and at changes begun in our strength. We dance to the harmonies of the universe and to the melodies within our own breasts. And we dream of unknown worlds on the strength of the world we know.

We stand as a people of faith, convinced not by the persuasion of our minds but by the experience of our lives. We are convinced that all is as you say it is—that you *do* number every hair on every head and see our every step.

We believe, O God. But when faith ebbs, we feel the pain of the world, and it spatters into the still waters of our lives. Infants die without drawing a breath. Wheat fields burn while standing ripe for the harvest. Old friends suffer diseases whose cures are years away. Tornadoes rip through the poorest sections of town. Innocent citizens are caught in the cross fire between governments. Workers lose the jobs they have held for years, while the unemployed have been turned away so many times they have traded hope for tears. And the children— abused because they wear the wrong color skin, speak the wrong language, live under the wrong flag, worship the wrong god—have no hope to lose.

The list is long, O God. But, somewhere in the midst of our sorrows, you are walking, holding hands, lifting up, mending wounds, breathing new life, and receiving the old. This we believe, and in this belief we find strength to remember and respond.

You have numbered us from the first to last. We pray that you might grant us the compassion to count one another daily. Let us reach to those who stumble, and break their fall; to the fallen, and pull them to their feet. Let us be caught when we are about to faint; and be lifted up, when we are struggling to rise.

✤ *Sunday Between June 26 and July 2.* Gracious God, you have not left yourself without a witness in any age or place. Wherever people have walked this earth, you have taken up residence among them and unveiled yourself to them. To Jacob you revealed yourself at the ford of the Jabbok. Even though he had deceived his father and betrayed his brother, you did not hide your face from him. To the Galileans you revealed yourself in Jesus' treatment of harlots and publicans. Upon perceiving that they were unworthy, Jesus showed them a love that would not let them go. We thank you, O God, that you do not hide yourself from the people who seem to merit your love. But we are even more grateful for your revelation to those who do not. We adore you, O God, for as the heavens are higher than the earth, your love is greater than our love. You shower it, like the rain, upon the just and the unjust. And you have given us in Jesus not only a summons to love as you love, but an example of both what it means and what it costs.

We long to love others as you do, but we seldom do. And our offense is compounded by the fact that we know better. We know that love can turn enmity into friendship, bitterness into acceptance, suspicion into understanding, and hostility into peace. But the love we would show to others we do not, and the hostility we would not show to others we do. Forgive us, O God, for bearing such shabby witness to you and for betraying our neighbors and ourselves.

Remind us of the love of Jesus Christ with which you claimed us as your own and we claimed you as our own. Rekindle in us the oneness we experienced when we accepted your invitation to join you in covenant. And let us go forth, renewed and empowered, to enlarge the circle of your covenant people. Make us quick to greet hesitation with generosity, suspicion with acceptance, anger with gentleness, and defensiveness with friendliness. When people ask us who we are, let us reveal whose we are.

The world in which we live suffers for want of many things. But the one thing it needs above all others is the love with which you have loved us and for which you call us to become channels. Give us, O God, the will and the wisdom to heed this summons.

❄ *Sunday Between July 3 and July 9.* How marvelous is the imagination of your eyes and the creation of your hands, O God! You have hidden truths from the world's wisest and most understanding creatures. Yet you reveal them to children—to those who see the unexpected and dream the unimagined, to those who play hide-and-seek with worldly logic and contemplate questions the world would forget.

Teach us, O Spirit, that the child in us must listen for your voice. Let us hear it speaking to us as a friend, as a kindred spirit, as a childlike presence. Let us hear it asking us to sing when the world demands silence and to dance when the world commands us to sit still. Let us hear it calling us to laugh when the world directs us to be solemn and to cry when the world orders us to be callous. Let us hear it bidding us to question when the world courts our loyalty and to have faith when the world makes us falter.

Call to the children crouching in the far corners of our hearts; beckon to them, coax them from their hiding places. Tell them your will, and what you whisper to them in secret, we shall proclaim from the house-tops for all the world to hear.

❄ *Sunday Between July 10 and July 16.* We bow before you, O God, in awe of your creation. Its vastness staggers our imagination. Its beauty kindles our excitement. Its mystery defies our understanding. As Jesus spoke to the crowds in Galilee in parables, sometimes you speak to us in parables. Your words are loud and powerful, but their meaning is not always clear.

Yet we sense the heartbeat behind your handiwork. In Jesus you have revealed your face, and we are delighted by what we see. We see power restrained by goodness. We see nature guided by humanity. We see purpose directed by love. We thank you, O Great Communicator, for the revelation of yourself in Jesus. At first we thank you for lowering yourself to our level. But as we look more closely at Jesus, we see that, instead, you raised us up to your level.

We grow uncomfortable in your company. Our humanity drags us down again to the level from which we ascended. Unlike Paul, we break under the weight of today's problems. We are constantly on the lookout for the quick fix. When our neighbor speaks to us harshly, we answer in kind without pausing to ask why. When given a chance to close a quick sale on dubious terms, we promise to be more ethical next time. When some foreign people opt for a system different from our own, we are quicker to denounce their choice than we are to study their history.

For this rush to judgment, we ask your forgiveness, O God. We pray for the rebirth of patience, that we might think beyond our present circumstances. Give us the grace to weigh our actions in light of their consequences on people yet unborn and on people in other lands. Let us hope for a world that we cannot yet see—a world in which we are as quick to bestow freedom as we are to claim it—and grant us the courage to labor for the world of our hope.

When we think of the degree to which our hope exceeds our grasp, we also remember the multitudes who cling to hope because hope is all that remains. We pray, O God, that you will move us to act in their behalf, that both we and they might obtain the liberty of the children of God.

🍁 *Sunday Between July 17 and July 23.*   Spirit of power, you are patient and kind. You do not insist upon your own way but call us to it, if we dare. You bear all things, believe all things, hope all things, and endure all things. And your promise has come to us, that we, too, can bear all things, believe all things, hope all things, and endure all things, if only we will pray.

What a strange thing is prayer! Perhaps it is not a *thing* at all, but a *verb*—not a *way* of life, but the *living* of a way of life. Like Paul, we do not know how to pray as we ought; we do not know how to live as we ought. But, like Paul, we are assured that you will help us. You will not only help us find appropriate words and postures for addressing you, but you will give us the fullness of your presence.

How we want you to be with us, Spirit! You surround us, fill us, abide with us, turn us around, and carry us into directions never taken. Your presence takes us not by storm but by sighs too deep for words. You do not make demands from afar, but you place yourself among us. Indeed, you place yourself *between* us, that our loving of others might be a loving of you and that our failure in loving others might be a failure to love you.

How often we fail to love, Spirit! We who have been rejected turn our backs on outcasts; we who have been betrayed walk away from friends; we who have fled shut doors on refugees; we who have stood alone have no patience with rebels.

Reason with our minds, Spirit! Argue with our souls! Show us our lives in your mirror, then reveal to us a vision of our living the life of prayer! Help us to pray as we ought; hear us and answer us with sighs too deep for words!

❧ *Sunday Between July 24 and July 30.* O Lord of heaven and earth, bend low to hear our plea, for we approach you in weakness and in need. Although the rulers of earth derive their power from you, sometimes they do not wield it in your spirit. They treat their land as if they owned it. They treat their government as if they were answerable to no one. And they treat their people as if they were not your people.

We wish, O Lord, that we could say we deserve better. Occasionally we do, but usually we get what we deserve. We do not wield great power, but we often abuse the little power we have. We do not have many possessions, but we often use the ones we have for selfish purposes. And we often treat the people below us as thoughtlessly as we are treated by those above us. Deliver us and our leaders from the thirst for more power than we know how to use, from the desire for more possessions than we need, and from the will to become masters over rather than ministers among our neighbors.

We come before you, O God, a mixed multitude. Some of us carry the burden of declining health; others mourn the loss of friends or loved ones; others have suffered losses in the marketplace; and a few of us are addicted to substances that work us harm.

But these differences aside, we all have one thing in common. We need your enlightenment of our understanding, your strengthening of our will, and, above all, your guidance of our lives. We are not alone in this need. We have no problems that others do not face; we bear no pain that others do not share; we experience no losses that others do not suffer; and all of us know that tomorrow could be our last day on earth.

So we pray, O God, that you will make us sensitive to all our neighbors. Bring us near to them that, through us, they might be brought near to you. And bring them near to us that, through them, we might be brought near to you. Just as Jesus became one with you and you with him, make us one with one another.

❧ *Sunday Between July 31 and August 6.* O God of love and mercy, you are the refuge of our lives, our haven in a storm, our shelter when all about us spins and whirls in turmoil. When things fall apart, you are the calm center to which we hold, assured that nothing in all creation can separate us from your love.

This knowledge of you is not something we have gleaned from reading books; it is not something we have captured with our minds. Rather, it is something that experience has planted and nurtured in our souls; there the seeds have taken root and grown to touch the sky.

What we know about you is beyond what we can say. You are a God beyond all words, a Hope beyond all wisdom. In mysterious, hidden ways, you teach us the meaning of true strength. You grant us a vision of the mightiest trees, whose trunks have weathered many storms. Let us learn from them to bend and sway in fierce winds, lest we crack and split and crash to earth.

Reveal to us, Faithful One, the knowledge of when we must stand tall, and lend us the courage to know that we *can*. Reveal to us the wisdom to know when we must bend, and inspire us with the passion to know that we dare. Give us the strength to lead others to the calm center of our lives. There they will know, perhaps for the first time in their lives, a perfect love. There they will find, perhaps in the first place ever, a perfect peace. There they will feel, perhaps in a way unlike any other, a perfect hope.

Center of our lives, center our lives, that we might carry you to those whose lives are falling apart, who are lost in the storms, whose worlds are spinning and whirling about them. We *know* that nothing can separate us from your love. Help us help them take refuge in you.

❧ *Sunday Between August 7 and August 13.* Gracious Lord, you are nearer than hands and feet and closer than breathing, yet we are often conscious of a great gap between you and us. Like Jesus' disciples when he left them to ascend the mountain for prayer, we feel ourselves drifting out to sea, lost in a fog of self-doubt. We are glad, O God, that you are not only aware of our frailty but ready to come to us in the midst of it. Just as Jesus came down from the mountain to minister to his distraught disciples, you come to where *we* are and minister to us according to our need.

Help us to become as open to our neighbors as you are to us. All too often we have opposed our neighbors in your name. Piling error upon error, we have confused loyalty to you with pride in our own beliefs. We have accused our neighbors of attacking your altar because they would not worship at ours; of breaking your covenant because they interpreted it differently from us; and of persecuting your prophets because they did not honor *our* prophets. Forgive our arrogance, dear Lord, and let us remember him who assured his followers that those who were not against him were with him. Grant us the grace to be charitable in passing judgment on others, lest they judge us as narrowly as we judge them.

We pray for the world's rebels. Some of them are rebels without a cause; illumine them, that they might discover a purpose worthy of their rebellion. Others are rebels for *your* cause; reassure them, that they might know it is better to be right and fail than to be wrong and succeed. Still others are rebels *against* your cause; challenge them, that they might come to know you as the friend and not the enemy of change.

As we consider those who rebel against you, let us ask why. Did we leave unspoken the sympathetic word that could have inclined them to your word? Or was it the unsympathetic word that we did speak? Did we leave undone the act of kindness that would have revealed to them your work in us? Or was it the unkind act that we did perform? Whatever the reason, give us the courage to remove any stumbling block that we may have erected between you and your children.

None of us, O God, has strength equal to our need. But you can more than atone for our weakness. Bless us with your presence, guide us with your spirit, and strengthen us with your might. Then we shall not only find strength for our need but need for our strength.

✤ *Sunday Between August 14 and August 20.* Beloved God, how reassuring it is to know that when others send us away, you will not join them in rebuking us. You will not shut us out, run from us, remain silent, or speak a word without mercy. If our sin makes us untouchable, you will touch us. If the world could, it would crucify the life from your body for loving us so. But you are bigger than the world, and your life is more powerful than death. So, you touch us.

O God who lays hands on the diseased and distressed, we are under the bondage of so many demons it is impossible to number them. For some of us the demon is poverty, while others are bound by wealth. Some are invaded by pride, and others by their humility. Some are confined by illness, and others by their strength. The demons possess us, they fill our thoughts and guide our actions, they own us; we are their slaves. Free us! Burst our chains and set us at liberty! Then shall our power be released to rescue your people.

O God, we await your salvation with great hope, trusting your mercy. In Jesus Christ you visited the most untouchable of people, the most unclean of society. You healed their wounded spirits and diseased bodies, then you marveled at their faith. Lord, we recognize you! Heal *our* spirits and bodies, that you may marvel at *our* faith.

❈ <u>*Sunday Between August 21 and August 27.*</u>   O great and gracious Creator, your ways are indeed inscrutable and your judgments unsearchable. And your patience defies all understanding. Were we in your place, patience would soon yield to impatience. We would over-rule the wills of your rebellious children and turn them into servants of *our* will. We would set this world straight in short order.

We thank you, O God, for meeting us in our place; for respecting our human condition and for setting the world straight in your own way. Some think you could cut through our stubborn resistance as lightning fells a tree. Perhaps you could. But you rarely do. You prefer, instead, to employ gentler methods. You do not walk among us as Creator among creatures, but as creature among creatures. And you reveal yourself only to those of us who see heaven on earth; who, having sur-vived the earthquake, wind, and fire, still incline our ears and hearts to the still, small voice.[1] As we approach you, O God, in the name of Jesus Christ, let us behold the One to whom we listen, and let us heed the One whom we behold.

Let us heed your summons to personal repentance. By your words and example, you teach us that the narrow way of self-giving is the path to self-fulfillment, yet we keep to the broad road of self-seeking. You invite your disciples to become colleagues, but we begrudge them your love. You call us to shape the church around the spirit of the Lord, but we confuse it with brick and mortar. For this betrayal—of you, our neighbors, and your church—we ask your forgiveness. We implore you once again to break the silence with your still, small voice.

Finally, dear Lord, let us heed your call to intercession on behalf of our neighbors. We know that you perceive their needs before we ask you to meet them. But you do not lightly excuse our failure to ask, for you turn our very asking into answers. Our asking is the stuff from which you forge our oneness with one another and with you. So we ask you, dear God, to turn us, receivers of your gracious love, into givers.

---

1. Inspired by I Kings 19:11-12.

Let us be good stewards to those looking for their place in the Lord's house. Let us give them the key that unlocks the door in the name and spirit of the Lord.

❈ *Sunday Between August 28 and September 3.* Eternal Giver of gifts, like a devoted parent you provide for us. Like children receiving daily nourishment and comfort, our eyes shine with trust when they dwell on you. And like children opening presents in breathless anticipation, we burst with delight. You see perfectly what we need and what we do not. You know best how to provide.

And you agonize deeply when we run away like rebellious children and turn to other sources in search of more of what *we* want. You weep as you watch us abuse not only others but ourselves by our misuse of your gifts. To all the world we may appear to be successful, but you measure success differently. To you success is the living out of the life of faith. And no room is found in the life of faith for the hoarding of your gifts.

Like all children, we need to grow up, that we might become responsible adults. Help us become faithful stewards—not because we are frightened into conformity by your wrath, but because we are moved to obedience by your love.

You have richly bestowed your gifts upon us, O God. Help us uncover the treasures you have hidden within us. Inspire us to open them for the benefit of all.

❈ *Sunday Between September 4 and September 10.*
Gracious Lord of creation, you have made us one in our dependence on you and one another. You have so ordered existence that, through our fellowship with human beings, we discover our need for communion with you. We praise you, O God, for esteeming us so highly, endowing us so richly, and trusting us so fully. We are humbled by your willingness to take such great risks for our growth into mature human beings. We bless you for having seen in us more than we see in ourselves and for having done better by us than we do for ourselves.

You have called us to be your witnesses. All too often, we have failed your summons. Occasionally we have hated evil, held fast to the good, and been affectionately devoted to one another. Yet we have seldom been zealous in showing honor, patient in enduring tribulation, or generous in responding to our brothers and sisters. If we have remembered to rejoice with those who rejoice, we have forgotten to weep with those who weep. If we have denounced the flagrant abuses of those in power over us, we have winked at the vices of those who live around us.

For all these transgressions, whether of omission or commission, we ask your forgiveness, O God. But remind us of the high cost of your forgiveness, lest we forget the magnitude of the task to which you have called us. You have called us to preach the Good News to the poor. Yet the world swarms with the poor who have never heard the Good News. You have called us to liberate the oppressed. Yet half the world's people have never known life without oppression. You have called us to set the prisoners free. Yet we continue policies that condemn persons to a life of bondage. Renew within us, dear Lord, our commitment to the victims of the world's injustice.

Today we have been quick to seek your help against the world's injustice. Grant that, in the struggle for justice, we shall be as quick to offer you *our* help.

❧ *Sunday Between September 11 and September 17.*

O Lover of the unlovable, your voice soothes the trembling of lowly, forsaken spirits. Your fingers grasp the hands of desperate, lonely sinners. How strong is your love! How your arms long to pull us close in your embrace! Those who sorrow could weep there; those who are weary, sleep. Those who are silenced could speak there; those who are hungry, feast. Those who hate could find peace there; those who rejoice, jubilee.

But we resist your strong embrace, clinging to the world. You ask us to break the world's grip, not by fleeing from it, but by staring it down. Dare the world with the mind of Christ, you say! Lock arms with your brothers and sisters to resist its power! *You* know, O God, whose spirit shall triumph! The spirit of wisdom and understanding, the spirit of counsel and might, the spirit of knowledge and love for the Lord!

O Forgiver of the unforgivable, receive us into your presence. Lift us from our knees that we might see you face to face. We have no right, but you give us all rights. We are not equal, but you love us equally. Let us who have been forgiven muster the strength to forgive. Let us who have found mercy find the compassion to be merciful. Let us who have yielded to peace yield our pride to be peaceful. Let us who have looked into the eyes of love see the way to be loving.

You are the Creator of the beautiful, O God. Change us! Change us, and we will forgive *before* being forgiven! Change us, and we will be merciful *before* seeking mercy! Enter us and dwell within us, that all the world may know who walks its roads and loves its people!

❧ *Sunday Between September 18 and September 24.*

God of the ages, whose hand led all the generations before us, we bow in gratitude for our rich heritage. Many of these generations did not have the wisdom of the ages on which to rely. Yet they were far from alone in the world, for they could rely on something even better than the wisdom of the ages. They could rely on the *God* of the ages. Thanks be to you, O God, for you did not abandon them in their search for life's meaning and purpose. And, thanks be to you, their search was not in vain. You gave them laws for their journey through the wilderness into a settled land. You sent prophets among them as they moved from the open country into crowded cities. Then, as science produced one revolution after another, you turned scientists into philosophers to warn us of the danger of pursuing progress without regard for purpose; of seeking wealth without respect for wisdom; of increasing power without concern for justice; and of improving technology without compassion for people.

You have taken pains to warn us of the dangers facing us, but we have often ignored your warnings. You dispatched prophets and apostles to remind us of the connection between love for you and love for your children. You made them partners with us in the gospel of reconciliation, but we have preferred to honor ourselves. We have praised partnership with our lips, but practiced individualism in our lives. Deliver us from our contentious ways and ambitious habits. Restore our oneness with you that we might rediscover our oneness with our brothers and sisters in Christ and, indeed, with all creation.

We are truly sorry, O God, for the damage we have done your cause in the world. We have failed you and, as a consequence, we have also failed our brothers and sisters. For this betrayal of you, of them, and of ourselves, we humbly beg your forgiveness. We ask you to renew in us the joy of our salvation. Grant us a fresh vision of our neighbors and ourselves as creatures fashioned in your image. Then, dear God, send us forth to perfect that image.

❧ *Sunday Between September 25 and October 1.*

Pathmaker of the universe, your way is straight, your way is narrow! It is the way of the just, the road that begins at the home of compassion and arrives at the threshold of mercy. You did not learn right and wrong sitting on a parent's knee or listening to a teacher or memorizing commandments. You *are* what is good; you ever have been and forever shall be.

Yet we insist on being your accusers. We question your presence and distrust your love. We believe our ways more just, our methods more sure, our feelings more deep. Our anger finds fault with you for finding fault with us. And you *do* find fault with us. But, Author of Life, your word of grace is spoken so simply. "Turn," writes the prophet, "and live!" "Repent," cries the Christ, "for the kingdom of God is at hand!" Your word sets before us a choice between life and existence.

At first glance, it appears to be an easy choice. But the abundance you promise is not the worldly abundance of which we so often dream. It is not displayed in property or propriety. Rather, your abundance is unearthed in the richness of paradox. It is an abundance found by persons who find their lives by losing them. It is an abundance found by those who gain their freedom by being captives. It is an abundance found by those who become right-side-up in your sight by living upside down in the view of the world. It is an abundance found by those who see the greatness of God revealed in the death of a criminal.

O God, you ask us to choose between life and existence. Contrary to appearances, the choice is *not* easy, for the life you offer is unlike any we have ever seen—except on a cross. You do, indeed, offer a life rich in paradox. It is a life demanding faith. Yet we often have only a kernel of faith when we stand in need of a giant redwood. We are not strong; redeem our weakness. We are not wise; transform our folly. We are not courageous; convert our cowardice.

Transfigure us, O Lord, for our personalities are split between yearnings for heaven and longings for earth. Give us daily glimpses of your abundant life, that we might daily risk stepping out of our mere existence into the unknown. We would turn and live, if we could. With you, O God, we can.

❧ *Sunday Between October 2 and October 8.* We address our prayer to you, O Life of the world. You are the planter; you are the seed; you are the sun; you are the rain; you are the harvest. Your hand holds in its palm beginnings without end; your heart hopes for ends that are eternal beginnings. Your eye dreams of nature's wealth, and behold,

it stands before you; and it is good. Your heart sighs for human companionship, and behold, they walk beside you, male and female as you have imagined them; and again, it is good.

Those of us who plant, those of us who dream, the ones who feast their eyes on the farthest horizons and chase the wildest sunsets—they are so like you! No wonder that Paul urges us to "press on!" Let us be grasped by the Spirit that was in Jesus, driving him to a life unimaginable. "Press on!" he writes. Let us forget what lies in the past if it keeps us from the future. "Press on!" he cries. Let us strain, *stretch* toward the mark, toward that chalk line God has drawn on the track. "Press on!" And the goal, always just beyond our reach, shall make us dig a little deeper, push a little harder, lift a little higher, give a little more to make the prize our own.

O God, you have such plans for us. Help us see our lives with your heavenly vision, that our earthbound eyes might see our higher calling. Let us examine ourselves in earnest; let us hold true to what we have attained; and let us resolve to mature under the loving care of the Spirit. Not that *our* race might be won, but that your will might be done.

❈ *Sunday Between October 9 and October 15.* O Maker of peace, on your people pour your power! Yours is a peace that passes all understanding. It is unlike ours. While we ignore distant battles to pretend that peace reigns, your peace assaults the violence of the nations. While we pen treaties with one hand and flash swords with the other, you smash economies driven by warriors and tend the wounds of their victims. While we slander our neighbors to their back and remain silent to their face, you pronounce judgment upon deceit and whisper comfort to the deceived. While we cry, "Peace, Peace," when there is no peace, you proclaim peace through the cries of a baby and ask us to believe.

How great is your peace, O Lord of creation! How small is our vision! We so easily dismiss Isaiah's vivid portrait—of the wolf dwelling with the lamb, and the leopard with the kid, and a little child leading them. We so quickly let go of Isaiah's vision of the feast on the holy mountain—with all the people of the world hosted by a God wiping away the tears from their faces. O Forgiver of the faint, we so timidly abandon your boldly painted dreams for creation! And we so strongly cling to the bloody nightmares of a desperate world!

O Maker of peace, on your people pour your power! Show us your strength, a strength that is not measured in numbers but embodied in *the* number: *One.* One God, who alone is worthy of our loyalty and our service; one God, who alone was with us in the beginning and shall be with us in the end; one God, who alone shall take us up in joy and lead us forth in peace. Then the mountains and the hills shall break forth into singing, and all the trees of the forest shall clap their hands.

Great is your peace, O God, and greatly to be praised!

❧ *Sunday Between October 16 and October 22.* You are God. There is no other. Created by you out of nothing, without you we return to nothing. You are the wind that lifts the wings of the birds; you are the wave that carries the salt to the sand. You are the song that bears glad tidings of joy; you are the voice that whispers across prairie and mountain. You are the God who does these things; truly, there is no other.

These things we know. But sometimes we are battered by winds unbroken and flooded by waves untamed. We hear music that lulls our goodwill to sleep and words that deceive us with the sweetness of honey. Then we turn our loyalties to little gods. Broken by our fears, we kneel at the altars of power and wealth, pride and ambition, privilege and self.

We soon forget, Lord, that you have knit our limbs together and made our minds to dream. Reclaim our bodies as your own, turn our thoughts into thoughts of you. And let us see those little gods for what they really are: lifeless puppets, sprawled limp on the ground, whose dance is death without our help. But you—you are the one who dances unhindered, despite our attempts to pull your strings. We cannot choreograph your movements, O God; so move us to do yours.

Let us move according to your will, and we will come alive. Make us captive to your spirit, and we will be free. The strings that bound us to the puppet-gods shall fall from our hands; our arms shall reach for the sun, and your breath shall lift us in flight. Then all will know that you are God, and you alone.

❧ *Sunday Between October 23 and October 29.* Listen, God of the Universe. Listen.

Hear the rhythms of creation dancing, rippling, spinning, resting, exploding among us. We are the people of creation. Listen to us.

You will hear tender voices whisper as a child is tucked into bed.

You will hear a tired spirit whimper as a street-dweller drops to sleep. You will hear strong fingers squeaking on violin strings. You will hear black knuckles breaking under a white soldier's boot. You will hear hearts leaping as a beloved draws near. You will hear memories groaning as an old friend makes friends with death.

Listen, O God, and you will know us. You will know us as a sometimes loving, sometimes lonely, sometimes talented, sometimes vicious, sometimes compassionate people. You will hear and know us as we really are, and love us as only you—our Creator—can love.

Your love for us will open the way for our life of faith, for life fulfilled in your greatest commandments. Your love will mine the gold of our hearts; it will dig deeply into our souls and tunnel through our minds. Then we will love you with all our heart and soul and mind. Your love will pierce into our hidden selves and let the light shine in. And then we will love our neighbors as ourselves.

We listen to you, Giver of the law of love. We hear a law spoken that is not a law but a link, not a commandment but a connection, not a rule but a relationship. We will hear, and know you, and then we will love you as only we—your creatures—can love.

❀ *Sunday Between October 30 and November 5.* Maker of dawn and dusk, of morning sun and evening star, how countless are your faces! They are not like masks, donned according to whim, taken off and put on to confuse all who behold you. No, they are like the colors splashed across the western sky at sundown. Their brilliance arrests the eye and lifts the heart, and the sunset needs them all.

Since time began you have painted sunsets with the shades of Eden. You capture our attention by constantly reappearing with faces as different as they are the same. Sometimes you are Creator; sometimes Mother, Father, Friend. Sometimes you have been Lover; sometimes Prophet, Ruler, Guide. But with whatever face you appear, you always encourage us—charge us—to lead a life worthy of you.

To lead a life worthy of *you*. We flinch at the task. Some of us do not know ourselves or our neighbors well enough to do as you ask; we drift away. Many of us know ourselves and our neighbors too well; and we despair. We are capable of great evil, both in what we do and what we do *not* do. We are also capable of great good, but often the need of our neighbor seems even greater.

O God, turn your gracious face and look upon us with love and understanding. Endow us with a humble spirit that is yet confident enough to answer your bidding. We are afraid of your face; we peer at it from a distance, hesitant to come near. Teach us that we cannot love you, ourselves, or our neighbors from afar.

Show us how to be worthy of you, God! You who mix the colors we see, author the words we speak, and create the good we seek, reveal yourself! And from the rising of the sun to its setting, your face shall be seen upon all the earth!

❧ *Sunday Between November 6 and November 12.*

O God, you are the Great Comforter. When the world around us turns cold, we feel you blanketing us with your love. Our lives are tied to yours, knotted together through thick and thin. How near you are! How constantly there! You are so near, so constant, so faithful to us that sometimes our faith in you becomes all too comfortable. We no longer strain to hear your "cry of command, the archangel's call" and "the sound of the trumpet of God."

You told us in Jesus Christ that the kingdom of God is at hand. Sent by you, that Word of yours sent us scurrying and crawling, grumbling and rejoicing. Not all of us took off running toward you or began singing your praises, yet few of us stood still with our hands in our pockets. But today, we think little about what is "at hand." We are too busy trying to keep things from getting *out of hand—our* hand. And you know only too well how miserably we fail at *that.*

Help us return to your way of looking at life: life on the move toward a point you have plotted, life on the brink between yesterday and tomorrow, life on the edge of a divine vision, life on the *other* hand— the right hand of God.

Your kingdom *is* at hand, O God. It is here, seen dimly, as if in a clouded mirror. Let us take up the cloth and wipe away the mist. Let us behold your kingdom in all its glory and embrace it with all our hearts, finding strength and comfort in the palm of your hand.

❧ *Sunday Between November 13 and November 19.*

God for all days and all seasons, hear our prayer! God for all nations and all peoples, listen to our voice! Constantly you hearken to cries of anguish in the night and shouts of rejoicing in the day. Again and again you are roused by lamentations in hidden places and clamorings in the streets. And you do not ignore quiet words falling on your ears.

Our prayer springs from burning hearts. We would like to believe Paul's words; we want desperately to be children of the light, but too long we have belonged to the night. Sometimes we walk in our sleep, not caring what happens around us. Sometimes we commit twisted deeds in this shadowy world through which we walk. Though we have pledged our loyalty to the light, the dark nights of the soul continue to haunt us. Day and night wage their war on the battlefield that lies within us.

O God, you are our hope! Awaken us from our sleep. Rescue us from the clutches of gloom. Reassure us in our fear and help us to become children of the light. Clothe us with the armor of faith and love, and give us for a helmet the hope of salvation. Bring that salvation to your children—to those who dwell in the day and to those who dwell in the night—that none might perish in the darkness.

We pray this in the name of the One who was the Way, the Truth, and the Light.

❧ *Last Sunday After Pentecost.*   Life: a one-syllable word loaded with mystery. And that mystery is you, O Creator of life, who in Christ shares life with the world!

"In Christ shall all be made alive." Hearing these words tempts us to count ourselves among the living. We forget that we are still sinners, and that within us rage those same forces that drove Paul against the Christians—the same pride in our convictions, the same inability to hear a different voice, the same insensitivity and even inhumanity to our fellow creatures and to creation.

Make us, like Paul, alive in Christ and dead to self, that we might become alive to the world. Enable us, once again, to hear the truth even when spoken by an uncommon voice; to respect the faith even when expressed in an uncommon way; and to discern the gospel even when revealed in an uncommon life.

Let the Damascus road be as real for us as it was for Paul. Awaken the compassion that sleeps in our breasts, that we too might be turned from persecutors into liberators.

Heal our sight, Lord, even as you lifted the scales from Paul's eyes. And let us follow your light into the pursuit of new missions and new visions. Let us die daily to self, that we might be resurrected to new life in the service of Christ and neighbor.

Year B

O Lord,

On this first Sunday of Advent, memories of Christmases past flood our souls. We recall the first time we heard the stories—the journey of Mary and Joseph, the praise of the shepherds, the music of the angels, and the lure of the star. These stories had an earthly ring, but they sounded a heavenly anthem. And like the shepherds, we praised you for revealing yourself in a manger.

Surprise us again, O Lord, as you surprised us in those days. Let this Christmas come to us, as that first Christmas came to the shepherds, and we will echo their song of thanksgiving in the name of Jesus.

We do not make this request as servants worthy of praise but as defendants deserving rebuke. When our prayers go unanswered, our eyes accuse not ourselves but you. And when our plans go awry, our hearts indict not our ambitious pride but your cold indifference. Yet we stand before you with confidence, O God, assured that you begin the search for us before we begin the search for you.

We pray that, as we await your coming *this* year, we shall do so with hearts yielded and minds chastened. Prepare us for a holy surprise. If you arrive at some other hour than eleven o'clock or some other day than Sunday, let us hearken to the song of your annunciation. And if you appear not in our sanctuary but in a shelter for the homeless, let us hasten to the site of your visitation.

When you came into Nazareth of Galilee, it was not merely to comfort but also to command, not solely to bless but also to judge, not alone to serve but also to rule. Even so, Lord Jesus, enter our world again. Surprise us as only God can—that, through you, we may come to God as, in you, God comes to us. *Amen.*

❧ *First Sunday of Advent*

Advent Season

❧ _Second Sunday of Advent._   Almighty and everlasting God, you have ordained every time as a time of preparation for the coming of Christ. Yet we need the challenge of Advent to prepare for his birth. As with gratitude we recall his coming to first-century Jewry, let us with joy anticipate his coming to twentieth-century Christendom.

Deliver us from the temptation to turn this Christmas into just another Christmas. The season's commonplaces—the hanging of the greens, the lighting of the candles, the singing of the carols, the giving of the fruit baskets—have all too often become a mindless routine, engaging our purses rather than our hearts, calling attention to our diligence rather than our devotion. Forgive us, O God, for allowing this holy day to become a mere holiday, for letting eternity's invasion of time become an occasion for time's corruption of eternity, for permitting your symbol of divine self-giving to become our sanction of human self-seeking.

Grant us penitent hearts, dear Lord, that we might become bearers as well as receivers of your comfort. Let us make common cause with those for whom Christ's coming turns bad news into good news: captives in a strange land, strangers in their native land, the neglected poor, the abandoned young, the forgotten elderly, the desperate lonely—all those who have fallen victim to humanity's _in_humanity. O Holy Comforter, as you break once again into our midst, make us channels of your consolation. Proclaim your healing word through our surrendered lips. Manifest your transforming presence through our yielded hearts. Work your gracious deeds through our outstretched hands.

As we travel again the road to Bethlehem, let us not forget that Golgotha is our destination. Keep ever before us the connection between the cradle and the cross, lest we mute the glory of Christ's coming and repeat the shame of his going. As we listen to the song of the angels, let us remember the message of Calvary. With an eye toward Jerusalem, let us march to Bethlehem, coming to the Lord as the Lord came to us.

❧ _Third Sunday of Advent._   O Eternal God, we bow before you, our Creator, in awe and gratitude. The grandeur of your majesty overwhelms us. Yet we adore you even more for the constancy of your love.

You do not need us as we need you. Yet you seek us before we seek you. Indeed, it is _because_ you seek us that we seek you at all. So it has been from the beginning of time. And so it shall be until the end of time. For this, dear Lord, we thank you.

Yet we come before you with mixed emotions. Guilt intrudes upon our gratitude, and we are moved to confession. Even though we know better, we insist on setting the terms for our relationship with you: We substitute our lineage for your love in drawing the boundaries of our community; we flatter those who praise us even though they may not praise you; and we recruit you in the service of our mission instead of enlisting ourselves in the service of your mission.

Deliver us from our double-mindedness, O God, that we may pursue you with the devotion of the shepherds, praise you with the song of the angels, and present you with a gift even greater than the gifts of the wise men—the gift of ourselves.

As we offer ourselves upon your altar, dear Lord, we do so for the sake of your mission and not ours. We are grateful for all those who bear your cross with us. They do not make the task easy, but they do make it easier. So we pray for the increase of laborers in your vineyard. May the coming of Immanuel so transform the members of Christ's body that you, through us, shall overcome evil with good: moving the well-fed to care for the ill-fed, the strong to rescue the weak, the devout to commune with the indifferent, the well to minister to the sick, the learned to teach the ignorant, the natives to accept the refugees, and the haves to remember the have-nots.

O God, as we await the coming of Christ into the world, we pray for the courage to embrace his mission *in* the world.

❧ *Fourth Sunday of Advent.*   Gracious God, from whom we receive the gift of life, in whom we learn the meaning of life, and to whom we owe the glory of life, we praise your holy name. We praise you for Jesus, who embodied human life that we might embody divine life.

We remember the story of Jesus' birth. Deep darkness shrouded the world, yet the light shone in the darkness, and the darkness did not overcome it. The violent did not abandon their weapons. The covetous did not surrender their ambitions. The wealthy did not share their possessions. The powerful did not honor their positions. The pious did not bother with their confessions. But your light, shining in the darkness, revealed the bankruptcy of violence, the futility of envy, the poverty of riches, the debauchery of power, and the hypocrisy of false piety.

We have seen your light, O Lord, yet we continue to walk in the shadows. We doubt that, in the nuclear age, a successful war can ever be waged, but we spend dollars for defense and pennies for peace. We recognize that, on an overcrowded planet, mass poverty threatens the rich and poor alike, but the gap between them widens and deepens. We realize that, in a world come of age, the divorce of religion from life would spell the death of religion, yet the link between divine worship and human service grows weak.

Of this betrayal of your will, we wish we could plead innocence. But we know that you know our guilt better than we. So we approach you with penitent hearts, seeking your illuminating presence. Let the light that shone in Bethlehem shine in our world. Let it burst into flames and consume the rage that pits us one against another.

O God, as we survey the world that awaits its savior, lift the scales from our eyes that we might behold the people for whom Christ became flesh. And take from us our hardness of heart, that we might see that, for them, *we* were born. As the Word became flesh *for* us, let the Word become flesh *through* us.

Christmas Season

❉ *Christmas Eve/Day.*   O God of creation, you cause the heavens to be glad and the earth to rejoice. You inspire the seas to roar and the fields to exalt. At your approach all the trees of the wood sing for joy, for they know that you come as no other comes: You come as righteousness and truth.

You come as the God of creation, and you remain as the God of the chosen. Who are the chosen? They are the Marys and the Josephs, who, when you come upon them, find that they cannot easily return to their own city; that their place in the world has been redefined; that they will receive new life not in a mighty house, not even in a humble inn, but in a wretched stable. Who are the chosen? They are the shepherds, who, when your glory appears around them, discover that they can no longer regard their fields and their flocks in quite the same way; that their place in the world has been redefined; that their hope will lie not among the Caesars, as they had always been told, but among the animals.

Who are the chosen? O God, they are those who, hearing your song in the heavens, seek your presence on earth. They are those who, locating the child, locate their own new place in the world. They are those who recognize that your grace appears for the salvation of all.

We are your chosen ones, O God. We are no longer alone. Our place is no longer what it was. For unto us a child is born; unto us an heir is given.

To this wrinkled, crying baby we would give the world, but the child has already claimed it for you. To this little, wriggling one we would give our future, but the child has already laid it in your hands. What, then, is left to give but the song ringing new in our hearts:

> O come, Desire of nations, bind
> All peoples in one heart and mind;
> Bid envy, strife, and quarrels cease;
> Fill the whole world with heaven's peace.
> Rejoice! Rejoice!
> Emmanuel [has] come to thee, O Israel![1]

❉ *First Sunday After Christmas.*   This very hour we give thanks to you, O God. For on this day we who have seen much

---

1. From the hymn "O Come, O Come, Emmanuel."

with our eyes have seen *all* with our hearts. We who have seen the dusk of so many old days have seen the dawn of a new day.

We, O God, have seen our salvation.

We could easily have *not* seen. Not because of tired eyes, but because of weary spirits. Time violates the heart; the advance of years breeds the anxieties of age. Oh, to be children again! To be cradled in the arms of our fathers, to be lifted by the arms of our mothers! To be strangers once again to our parents' world!

But our childhood has vanished. We have grown, becoming strangers to one another and to ourselves. We have grown, becoming wise in the ways of our parents' world and feigning ignorance of the ways of your world.

We were groping for your new world, O God. In some remote corner of our foolish hearts, we were hoping for your salvation—but *this* is not what we expected. You sent no armies of angels to fight our fights, no yellow-brick roads to show us the way, no earthquakes to topple our great walls of fear. No, to save us, you sent what we had lost: You sent the child into our hearts, and we lifted the child into our arms and blessed your name.

This child is only one of many born among us, only one of many you have called holy, only one of many we have seen. Yet this child, whom we have seen *with our hearts,* has brought joy to all the world.

Still, our joy is pierced with great sorrow, for this child shall not remain a child. Surely he shall grow and become strong; he shall be filled with the wisdom of the new world. But when the child enters *our* world—Savior, we shudder to know that we shall rob him of his youth; that we shall sacrifice him upon ungodly altars. "Unto us a child is born," yes; but unto whom is this child given? Into whose hands, O God, have you commended his spirit? Are they ours, Lord? Is it we who have received him, only to give him up for thirty pieces of silver?

O God, return Mary and Joseph and Jesus safely to their own city. Be with them; watch over the Child as the days pass, but slow Time's course. Help us to prepare for him, to make straight our ways! Help us, before the hour is late, to bless, not curse; to declare, not deny; to trust, not betray; to be reborn, not to die. Help us, O Lord, to keep the child within us safe, lest we destroy the child you sent to save us.

❦ *Second Sunday After Christmas.*   Long have we been in exile, O Lord; long have we been lost from the land of our birth. By the rivers of strange cities, the cities of our enemies, we have sat down and wept, remembering that place where once we lived—a safe place where despair was a stranger. But now *we* are the strangers in a strange land, and mocking waters flow quietly by, undisturbed by our troubles.

Shall we sing the Lord's song in a foreign land? Shall we sing the Lord's song at our captors' command? O, but how temptation sometimes tears at us as we stand before those who have hurt us! How the words torture our throats! How we, with the psalmist exiled in Babylon, would spit at our tormentors, "Happy shall be the one who dashes your children against the rock!"[2] Yes, we would sometimes save ourselves, sometimes heal ourselves by meeting cruelty with cruelty, hatred with hatred, death with death!

But from the Child have we received, grace upon grace; from the Child has the world received, grace upon grace upon grace. We and the world have received our redemption; embracing the babe, we embrace our salvation. In the Child's presence we weep with our enemies—first for shame, then for joy—for, from Bethlehem and Babylon and beyond, the Lord has gathered us together.

Together we shall walk by brooks of water, in a straight path on which we shall not stumble, for the Child shall lead the way.

Together we shall sing aloud on the heights, in a lofty place from which we shall not fall, for the Child shall sit among us.

Together we shall feast on the fatted calf, at a table from which we shall not be barred, for the Child shall break the bread and pour the wine.

And together we shall bid the little children come unto us, these children who might have suffered our spite, for the Child shall play among them.

Together we shall be led back, O God, and of you we shall be born again.

---

2. See Psalm 137:9.

Season After Epiphany

✤ *Baptism of the Lord: First Sunday After Epiphany.*
O God, your ear hears the songs of the universe before they are sung, the symphonies before they are played, the harmonies before they are sounded. As your voice hums the lyrics of the canticle you have composed, your ear tunes the strings of the lyre you have crafted. You are composer, conductor, musician, and music, and you have created us to read the score, to follow your direction, to sing to your accompaniment, to dance with the Word.

Thus we know you. Your voice has sung to us, and its song is familiar. It rises in the majesty, falls in the agony, rushes in the ecstasy, and rests in the serenity known by your creatures. Sometimes, when we hear the rise and the fall, the rush and the rest, we begin—despite ourselves—to hum along with you. You glory in the entrance of our voices, and you lead us in the concert of creation.

We strain to hear your Word, O God, and you strain to hear our word. If we yodel from the heights of joy, you echo our song. If we wail from the depths of despair, you join our lamentation. If our voices peal in exaltation, you ring with them. If our voices pause in expectation, you wait with them.

But sometimes we are not so faithful as you are, Lord. We are tempted to sing solo, to disrupt the flow of the song, to refuse to sing altogether. We head out into the desert to chant with lonely voices to the sands, and, although we are met by their silence, we would rather sit alone among the shifting dunes than stand with the chorus upon the rock.

But even when our words are not your words and our ways are not your ways, even when isolation tempts us to destruction and exultation surrenders to lamentation, your voice sends out the Word into your world. It stands before the entrance to the tomb, it edges near the threshold of the void, and there it sings a love song to life. And, behold, life dances forth from the grave, leaping to the rhythms of the universe.

We praise you, O God, for making your Word the Word of life. For since the beginning your voice has promised that "as the rain and the snow come down from heaven, and . . . water the earth, making it bring forth and sprout, giving seed to the sower and bread to the eater, so shall my word be that goes forth from my mouth; it shall not return to me empty, but it shall accomplish that which I purpose, and prosper in the thing for which I sent it."[3]

❧ *Second Sunday After Epiphany.* O God of Hannah, mother of Samuel and woman of God, who so longed for a child that she could no longer pray in words, receive our prayer. Grant us peace. For like Hannah, we have been barren. We have hoped. We have labored. We have expected. We have trusted. But our hopes have faded, our labors have been lost, our expectations have fallen, our trust has been broken. Yes, Lord, we know Hannah well. Send us the peace that came to her, even before her discovery that she was with child.

O God of Eli, father of rebellious sons and priest of a rebellious peo-ple, who so longed for a word from the Lord that he would hearken even to a word from a child, receive our prayer. Grant us your light. For like Eli, we have been unseeing. We have wandered about in a darkness of our own making. We have stumbled upon the bricks and stones of our own laying. We have been terrified of strange sounds and retreated to our own beds. Yes, Lord, we know Eli well. Send us the presence that came to him through the words of the child of Hannah.

O God of Samuel, son of a barren woman and servant of the Lord, who so longed for the sight of you that he slept beside your lamp in the temple, receive our prayer. Grant us clarity of vision. For like Samuel, we have been confused. Voices shout, whisper, grumble at us from all sides. At the shouting we tremble, at the whispering we shiver, at the grumbling we shrink. Which voice is yours? Which one, ours? Which one, theirs? Which do we follow, which ignore? Yes, Lord, we know Samuel well. Send us the clear vision that came to him through the guidance of his blind friend Eli.

O God of Philip, man of Galilee, who so longed for Israel's deliver-ance that he rushed to tell Nathanael of the messiah's arrival, receive our prayer. Grant us courage. For like Andrew and his friends, we have been anxious. Who should be our leader? Many would rule us, many would teach us, many would tempt us. But the rulers' domination con-cedes little freedom. The teachers' instruction yields little enlighten-ment. And the tempters' persuasion offers little satisfaction. Yes, Lord, we know Andrew well. Send us the courage that came to him when he found where Christ was abiding.

---

3. See Isaiah 55:10-11.

O God, we are not our own. Our hearts are yours; fulfill them. Our hearts are yours; reassure them. Our hearts are yours; inspire them. Our hearts are yours; empower them. Transform them into your temples, and we will listen for your voice.

❧ *Third Sunday After Epiphany.*   O God, whose breath inspires life and whose heart beats in the womb of the world, how unfeeling we are! We fear the touch of your breath for it stirs the winds of change. We are numb to the rhythm of your heart for it brings the pangs of birth. When we feel, we fear, and we grow numb to the world that is our home. When we feel, we fear, and we grow numb among the creatures who are our family.

Release us, O God, that we may receive your spirit. Place our finger on the pulse of life. Transform us, and we shall know a world transformed: The ordinary shall become unusual, the routine shall become miracle. The time for loving shall seem short, and we shall love more ardently. The time for hating shall seem long, and we shall hate less fervently. We who have loved and lost shall find; we who have hated and gained shall lose. The last shall be first, and the first shall be last.

Release us, O God, and unleash us to do the work of the kingdom. Bid us rise, and send us even to those places that we consider defiled, even to those persons we consider unclean. Show them, through us, that your love may purify. And show us, through *them,* that we, too, must be purified.

Some of us, no doubt, will try to run away from the mission on which you send us. Wanting *comfortable* missions and *safe* visions, among our own kind and in our own place, we will board a ship heading in the opposite direction from where you would have us go. But you are persistent, God. If we flee, you will follow; swallowing us up, you will swim us back to shore, there to have us start again, there to give us another chance.

Some others of us will, no doubt, ignore you from the first and go on sitting in our boat, mending our nets. We will be all wrapped up in the old ways, and quick with excuses. We have spent our lives catching our fish, and we have caught them according to our own custom. And yet, to show us a new way, you raise up a *carpenter* to teach us. Why should we trust? Why should we risk?

But the winds of change are blowing. You breathe on us, commanding us, like Jonah, to love without passing judgment. You breathe on us, commanding us, like Zebedee, to change against our better judgment.

And, yes, the pangs of birth are pounding. The time is fulfilled, and the kingdom of heaven is at hand. We shall repent, Spirit, and, rising up in power, we shall lift Zebedee from his seat and carry him with us into the new age. If we have fear, we shall be born to courage; if we are numb, we shall awaken to awareness. Only let us *feel,* O God, and we shall care for this world that is our home. Only let us *feel,* and we shall love these creatures who are our family.

🍁 *Fourth Sunday After Epiphany.*

> Source and Sovereign, Rock and Cloud,
> Fortress, Fountain, Shelter, Light,
> Judge, Defender, Mercy, Might,
> Life whose life all life endowed:
> May the church at prayer recall that
> no single holy name
> but the truth behind them all
> is the God whom we proclaim.[4]

O God, we speak names for you, yet your name is unspeakable.

You *are* what we call you, yet you are beyond what mere words can say. You *are* what we know you to be, yet you are more than mere knowledge can comprehend.

But if your name is unspeakable, you are not unapproachable. Indeed, you approach *us,* an event so unthinkable, so unimaginable that we refuse to see you. You enter our presence and teach us. And while we are astonished at your teaching with such authority, we still do not recognize you. *We* do not, but the demons within us do. The evil within us acknowledges you as the Holy One of God, and you banish it from your presence. And still we are only amazed that a simple carpenter should command such authority.

You are a burning bush, Lord, but you are more than a bush that burns. Open our eyes when we see the bush, so that we cannot help taking off our shoes. You are a commanding word, but you are more than

---

4. From the hymn "Source and Sovereign, Rock and Cloud" by Thomas H. Troeger. Copyright © 1987 by Thomas H. Troeger. Reprinted by permission of Oxford University Press.

a master teacher. Open our ears when we hear the word, so that we cannot help taking up our bed and walking.

O God, your name is unspeakable, but we call upon you. Though you are beyond what mere words can say, our words rise to you. Though you are more than mere knowledge can comprehend, our minds reach for you. And more than any words or any knowledge, our hearts search for you, for they, too, would cry out with a loud voice, "I know who you are, the Holy One of God!" They, too, would say to you, "You are the Christ!" For you are

> Word and Wisdom, Root and Vine,
> Shepherd, Savior, Servant, Lamb,
> Well and Water, Bread and Wine,
> Way who leads us to I AM:
> May the church at prayer recall that
> no single holy name
> but the truth behind them all
> is the God whom we proclaim.[5]

❈ *Fifth Sunday After Epiphany.* O God, how you humble us! How you redefine our definitions, rendering our words obsolete by the activity of your Word! How you turn our world upside-down, showing the wisdom of our ways to be the folly of the ages! How you reveal our truths to be riddles, converting our answers into questions!

You are, indeed, the God of the psalmist. You, whom we claim to worship, are not impressed by the strength of a stallion or the might of a human arm. Yet we idolize the strong and the mighty among us, be they mortal or machine. We trust them to entertain and amuse us, guide and protect us. Their strength allows us to be weak; their might permits us to be meek. While we watch from the sidelines, their ambitions compete, struggling to the last gasp. We are impressed, and we are perplexed that you are not. We cannot understand why you would take pleasure in our love for you and one another.

If you are the God of the psalmist, then you are indeed the God of Paul, once named Saul. You are the God of that angry and zealous defender of religious tradition who could not tolerate new visions. You smote him as he rode his stallion down the Damascus road, waving a persecutor's sword in his mighty arm. You knocked him down, you

---

5. Ibid.

shone a light into his blinded, impassioned soul, and you said, "Saul, you do not know what you do." Your love for him set him in a new world and gave him a new name: Paul, become free, become slave to all. Paul, become Jew among Jews and Gentile among Gentiles. Paul, become weak among weak and strong among strong. Paul, become all things to all people, so that others might see the light, dismount their horse, and throw down their sword.

If you are the God of Paul, then you are indeed the God of Simon's mother-in-law. She was probably an aging widow, not highly regarded in her community or in her son-in-law's household. She was not strong, but ill; she was not mighty, but a woman in a man's world. Yet your Son, O God, did not pass her by. He touched her, and she became a woman healed, a woman freed; a woman who arose from her bed not to resume the ordinary way of doing things, but to *minister* unto others; a woman healed on the Sabbath, who arose to serve the Lord of the Sabbath.

Simon did not understand the reality that Jesus of Nazareth had brought to Capernaum. He chased after Jesus and interrupted his time of prayer to beg for more miracles. Lord, if you are the God of Simon, then you are our God, for we, too, fail to understand this kingdom that you have sent into our midst. Open our hearts, that we may perceive what is real, what is desirable, what is good. Show us again what strength is, and what might can do, if it is yours. Help us sing of it, as did the psalmist; to preach about it, as did the apostle; and to embody it, as did the disciple, who understood and served.

❧ *Sixth Sunday After Epiphany.*   O Lord, you are the Great Healer. You touch, you tend; you bathe, you bind up; you deaden pain, you awaken joy. Your touch is tender, your tending is careful; your bathing is thorough, your binding up is gentle; your deadening of pain is merciful, and your awakening of joy is continual. You nurse the broken, but even before you reach for us, *you have looked for us.* You have sought us, and you have seen us. That you, the Great Healer, are also the Great Seer—this may be the greatest miracle of all.

We are a talented people, Lord. We are given the capacity for making ourselves invisible, and some of us practice long and hard to develop that capacity. Over the years we fade into a transparent, ghost-like existence. We glide in and out of people's lives, brushing by them without being touched. We observe them without being seen. We eavesdrop on them without being heard. It is easier if we become invisible, Lord, because we fear being slapped down, we fear appearing foolish, we fear the penalty for speaking the truth.

We are also given the capacity for making other people invisible, and some of us work long and hard to develop *that* capacity. Over the years we sharpen our image at the expense of others. We become numb to their touch; we become blind to their presence; we become deaf to their cries. It is easier if we make them invisible, Lord, because their need makes demands on our power, their pain witnesses in the midst of our pleasure, and their world mocks the security of our own.

Forgive us our fear, O Healer. It would have us hide from your touch, the touch that would restore us to personhood. Forgive us our pride. It would have us deny that *our* touch could restore personhood to others. Forgive us for clamoring for miracles wrought by *your* hand, when you have laid the power to work miracles in *our* hands.

Paul writes about "running the good race." Lord, if we have fallen on the track, we pray for strength to struggle up and start running again. If we run but trip those next to us, stop us and have us lift them up. As we run, keep our eyes fixed not on a prize of this world but on a treasure of your kingdom on earth. Yours is a treasure imperishable, a trophy sanctified. It is a laurel that rests on the head inquiring into the truth, the heart searching for your will, and the hand reaching to the neighbor.

Let us leprous ones run to kneel before you, O Seer who will see us, that we might rise to run for you, O Healer who will heal us.

🍁 *Seventh Sunday After Epiphany.* Faithful God, we have never seen anything like you. You are the Promise, and you are the Keeper of the Promise. You are the sun sinking into a bath of color at the close of the day, and you are the orange dawn awakening us for another. You are the memory of last spring sustaining us through the long winter, and you are the warm thaw signaling a new beginning. You are the One who, to save a people hurling its no at your face, whispers the yes into its ear. You are the One who, to send a Savior to creation, delivers a baby unto the world.

No, we have never seen anything quite like you. But we *have* seen someone in your likeness. You have sent someone among us who is Faithfulness itself, and we have betrayed it. You have sent someone who is Forgiveness itself, and we have passed judgment on it. And in so doing we have betrayed you, and we have passed judgment on ourselves.

We have never seen anything like you, but we have seen *someone* like you. But we have driven him away, unable to bear the sight of him or the sound of his words. He walked into our midst proclaiming a new age, and *bringing* a new age, but we are comfortable with the old. Can it be that we do not really *want* to see anything like you, God? Can it be that we do not really want to hear your voice? If you are the Promise, the Promise that would change the world, can it be that we do not really want you to keep it? And if all your "promises find their yes in Christ," can it be that we do not really want the Christ to come?

Lord, forgive us for exacting faithfulness from you but not from ourselves. And pardon us for claiming that forgiveness can flow from you and you alone. Send us people, O God, whose faithfulness will help us become faithful, whose forgiveness will help us forgive. Send us people, O God, who shout "Amen!" to your Promise. Send us people, O God, who can bring us paralytics of the spirit into the presence of the holy, where our resolve can be strengthened and our bodies renewed. Then shall the world be amazed and glorify your name.

❧ *Eighth Sunday After Epiphany.*

> Beloved God, we seek you.
> Beloved God, we need you.
> Beloved God, we know you.
> Lover of souls, we would know you better.

When we are trapped in our folly, you whisper in our ear the way to freedom. When we are unfaithful, you court us with tenderness and lure us back to a familiar place, a fertile place that once we shared. There you kneel with us and prepare the soil for a pleasant planting. As we sift the earth through trembling fingers and smell its moistness and feel its warmth, you set the vines for the vineyards of your people. Reminding us of the past that we lived with you in this place, you plant our hope for the future.

Lover of souls, we would know you better.

When we are most unmerciful, you are Mercy. When we are least gracious, you are Grace. You are slow to anger; you pluck the sins from our confessing tongues and hurl them as far away as the east is from the west. You abound in a steadfast love that towers like the heavens above the earth; you scoop from the ground the evils our hands have wrought and fling them into the clouds.

And soon thereafter it always rains, and a rainbow arches over the fields. The rain waters are our evil made pure. They baptize our vineyard with life, for you do not desire that we eat sour grapes, nor that our children's teeth be set on edge.[6]

> Beloved God, we would know your name. Christen us.
> Beloved God, we need your power. Possess us.
> Beloved God, we seek your presence. Find us.

❧ *Transfiguration Sunday: Last Sunday After Epiphany.*
Lord, a prophet appeared in the wilderness, calling us to a baptism of repentance. And we went out to him, and we were baptized in the river Jordan, confessing our sin.

A man named Jesus also came. And when he waded from the water, we saw the heavens open and the sun stream through, but we thought only that the cloud cover had finally broken. And, too, it is said that a voice spoke from heaven, but we heard only a distant rumbling, like thunder rolling over the hills.

We remember that day, not because of the deep impression it made, but because this day has brought it to mind. Today we have seen and heard what then we did not see and hear. We have seen a man transfigured, and we have heard his name revealed. But with trembling we must confess: We understand little more this day than we did then.

We must also admit that the memory of our own baptism has faded. Its meaning has paled. For in our world "repentance for the forgiveness of sin" is a foreign language. "Pride in the pursuit of pleasure" is our native tongue.

Lead us up the high mountain, Lord, and transfigure us. At our baptism we pledged to you our souls, and we were reborn by the water. Now we pledge to you our very lives, that we may be reborn by the Spirit. We will hold nothing back, for nothing is ours to retain. At creation you made us in your image. Reshape us now in your likeness, for we have donned the masks of other gods. Our land is filled with them, and these we worship, the painted works of our own hands.[7]

---

6. Inspired by Jeremiah 31:29-30.
7. Inspired by Isaiah 2:8.

Clothe us in light, Lord, for we would be children of the light. Send to us your word, Lord, for we would be doers of the word. Lay on us your mantle, Lord, for we follow the One who wears the crown. Lord, we remember our baptism. May we receive our transfiguration.

Lenten Season

❦ *Ash Wednesday.* O God, from whom we are ever prone to stray but who always remains close enough to hear our cry for help, we approach you with a sense of shame and a sigh of relief. When we think of how little we have done with all you have given us, we are ashamed—ashamed of our deafness to your call to replenish the earth and tend it; of our failure to join our brothers and sisters in making our planet safe for humanity; and of our failure to practice our piety to be seen of God rather than our neighbors.

Despite our shame, we are relieved—relieved that you have not acted on the reasons we have given you for forsaking us; that you have not abandoned your creation or your reliance on your creatures; and that people are demanding a form of worship that puts less emphasis on form and more emphasis on worship. So we are not only relieved but delighted to be able to greet still another Ash Wednesday as a people who are still alive, still loved, and still yours.

We thank you, O God, that we can always count on you to deal with us, not according to our sin, but according to your mercy. Not over-looking our bent to falsehood, you demand that we pursue the truth. Not discounting our inclination for folly, you offer us a diet of wisdom. Not disregarding our thirst for peace of mind, you dispense the joy of salvation only to right spirits and pure hearts.

We wish, O Lord, that you could count on us as we count on you. But you know our record of transgression too well for us not to come clean. We earnestly and truly repent of our sin, and are heartily sorry for our transgressions. Remove them as far from us as the East is from the West. And create in us a heart within which they will never again find a home.

This is the day of the Lord! O Lord, proclaim to the people the Good News that your day is their day, too. Show us the stepping stones, one by one, with which Jesus marked the road that leads to you—the Jesus who faced every trial with which we could be tested, but was upended by none of them; the Jesus who was tempted by every vice to which we are vulnerable, but was subdued by none of them; the Jesus who was treated as if he were below our contempt, but who died as one above our reproach. Forgive us, O God, for having buried his stepping stones beneath our stumbling blocks. Create in us a clean heart and renew a right spirit within us, not only that we may walk in his shoes, but that we may add new stepping stones to those he has already laid.

❈ *First Sunday in Lent.*   O Lord and lover of us all, by whose power we stand and before whose goodness we bow, we praise you for your matchless patience. We have given you ample reason to turn away from us, but your face is turned ever toward us. Try as we may to make it on our own, you do not abandon us to our own devices. You come to us as a caring mother, wooing us home with open arms and challenging us with a love as persistent as it is pure. Even though we spurn you, you do not spurn us. And though our loyalty often wavers, your patience never wears thin.

We thank you, O God, for your patience. Not only does it overcome our anxiety; it exceeds your justice as well. If you dealt with us according to our just deserts, none of us could stand. Yet we address you in confidence and in hope, assured that your patience is a match even for our disobedience; assured that, while it may be late for our repentance, it is not too late for your forgiveness; and assured that, even though our love has let go of you, your love will never let go of us.

As we ponder this love, we are reminded of our calling to become its agents. This call has fallen on deaf ears and hard hearts. We have not so commended ourselves as your servants as to remove the obstacles in the way of our neighbors. We have strewn their path with so many obstacles that we leave them wondering just whose servants we really are. When adversity strikes, they are not surprised to hear from us cries of lament rather than hymns of fortitude. When opposition mounts, they are not surprised to see us fleeing the scene rather than standing our ground. But they are surprised, when we are afforded the chance to speak the truth in love, to find us willing to take the risk.

If we had given only our neighbors reason to be displeased, we would have ground for remorse. But in failing them, O Lord, we have also failed you. We have betrayed you, not only by the good deeds we could have done for our neighbors but did not. We have betrayed you also by the good deeds we did solely for their benefit: by the alms we gave to be noticed not by you but by them; by the prayers we mouthed to be heard not by you but by them; and by the fasting we endured to be witnessed not by you but by them.

For our sin, whether expressed in acts of omission or commission, we ask your forgiveness, O Lord. Give us a penitent heart, and fill us with an obedient spirit, that we might discern and do your will. Restore to us the joy of our salvation, that before our neighbors we might place not stumbling blocks but stepping-stones; and that we might, on the streets as in the sanctuary, become the agents of your mission.

O God, bring us and our neighbors together in a fellowship so compelling that we will proclaim your gospel as Jesus proclaimed it to the Galileans, saying, "The time is fulfilled, and the reign of God is at hand; repent, and believe in the gospel."

🍁 *Second Sunday in Lent.*　O God of Abraham and Sarah, Isaac and Rebekah, Jacob and Rachel, with deep humility we recall your covenant with our ancestors. No matter how much their faith wavered—and they all had moments of doubt and uncertainty—*you* remained ever faithful. No matter how often they broke covenant with you, *you* always kept covenant with them. As it was with them, so it is with us. The covenant is alive and well, not because of us but because of you. So we thank you, dear Lord, for judging us not justly but mercifully; for dealing with us not on the basis of our goodness but yours; and for coming to us not because you need us but because we need you. We praise your name for not forsaking us in our low estate, for stooping to us in our depths that you might lift us to your heights.

Yet our gratitude mingles with guilt. We bow in shame before the treachery of our ancestors. Then we pause to examine ourselves, and we are more ashamed than ever. For even with their mistakes plainly before us, we repeat them as if they had never been made. Even with their confessions clearly before us, we shelve them as if they had never been uttered. But in the end we learn, as they learned, that from your presence there is no hiding place; and that the hound of heaven will never stop running after us until we stop running from ourselves.

For this folly, O God, we beg your forgiveness. The breach between you and us is wide, but it is of *our* making and not yours. We are the transgressors, but we are not proud of our transgressions. We are especially sorry for duplicating the mistakes of our ancestors. Enable us now, O God, to put the sinful past behind us, theirs and ours, that we might embrace the hopeful future with confidence.

Raise our vision beyond our daily routine to the distant horizons of your sovereign rule. Let us no longer walk through the world as self-centered dreamers. Grant us the sensitivity of our Lord that we too might be moved from complacency to action. And let our action, like his, be rendered with an eye only to your will for the human family and without regard for personal risk to ourselves.

As we consider the summons of Jesus to deny ourselves, take up the cross, and follow him, let us remember this simple truth: For us as for him, crossbearing is a way of living before becoming a way of dying.

✤ *Third Sunday in Lent.* O God, who has endowed us with a thirst that you alone can quench, a hunger that you alone can satisfy, and a restlessness that you alone can still, we turn to you in adoration and prayer. We turn to you because there is no one else to whom we can turn, confident of finding answers to our questions and quiet for our souls. In vain we have looked elsewhere for succor. So now we seek you, counting on your promise that mourners shall be comforted, the weak strengthened, the foolish made wise, and crossbearers vindicated. We thank you, O God, not only for inviting us to call upon you in our hour of need, but also for receiving us not as beggars but as friends.

We do not deserve such a welcome. Our words and thoughts and deeds have raised a wall of hostility against you. You gave the law as a lamp unto our feet, but we have cast it into a weapon for attacking others. You delivered the Commandments as signposts for the way, but we have treated them as statutes for passing judgment. You entrusted us with the testimonies of your unmerited love, but we have twisted them into proofs of our superior virtue. You gave us the light that we might help others find the path of discipleship, but by refusing that light we have helped obscure it. By spurning your offer of communion, we have closed the channels of grace for others.

So we implore your forgiveness, O God, not only for our unwitting detours off the path of love but for all those whom we have led astray. Let us rediscover the transforming power of a faithful relationship with you, so that, instead of conscripting you into the service of our religion, we shall enlist our religion in your service.

As we reflect on our Lord's impatience with the moneychangers who turned the house of God into a house of trade, we cannot help sympathizing with the victims of his wrath. We too have been tempted to mistake the adornment of our sanctuary for the fulfillment of our mission. So we humbly pray, O God, that you will save us:

From assuming that a gift for the church is a gift for God;
From talking more about what people do for the church than about what the church does for people;

From taking greater pride in bringing the world into the church than in sending the church into the world;

From elevating the servants of your Word into rulers of our congregations;

From forgetting that we must sometimes oppose the prescriptions of religion for the sake of truth.

Help us this day, O Lord, to rediscover the church as the Body of Christ and ourselves as its members, each caring for the others and all working for you. Continue the work through this, your second body, that you began in Nazareth of Galilee.

🍁 *Fourth Sunday in Lent.*   O God, who in nature displays matchless power and who in Christ manifests marvelous grace, we bow before you in grateful adoration. We are moved to awe by your power; we are moved to shame by your grace. We rejoice in your goodness and your greatness. For if your goodness were as ours, you would not redeem us; and if your greatness were as ours, you *could* not redeem us. We thank you, O Lord of heaven and earth, that your goodness is equal to our need; that your greatness is a match for your goodness; that you can and do redeem us.

Like the Israelites in Babylon, we know what it is to live in a foreign land. But unlike the Israelites, *our* exile was not inflicted by others. We became exiles by choice. Even though we were made for you, we strayed from your path like lost sheep. Some of us joined the prodigal in the far country. And when our captors tormented us, saying, "Sing us the songs of Zion," we complied. We sang the songs of Zion to the tunes of life in the fast lane. Big bucks, easy virtue, selfish indulgence: These became our gods and defined our goals. But others of us, like the elder brother, became exiles from your presence at home. We did not travel to the far country, yet we became as estranged from you as if we had. We remembered Jerusalem, but only to rebuke it for not delivering the privileges we were promised. We still sang the songs of Zion to the old tunes, but we did it from habit and not from the heart. The church was never open when we were not there; the offerings were never taken that we did not contribute; helpers were never sought that we did not volunteer. We lamented the disregard of our studied piety: "Why," we asked, "are we not given the credit due us? And why, when the prodigals return home, is such a fuss made over them?"

No matter the class of prodigals to which we belong—whether the vagabond or the home-grown—we are homesick for your presence, O God. We are weighed down in bondage to the sin that sent us into exile, and we long to be free again. Pardon our iniquity, O Lord. Unfurl your mighty arm, deliver us with your victorious right hand, set our feet upon your path, and we shall walk in your way, heed your word, and obey your law.

As we return home to you, O Lord, we are mindful of the multitudes who grope in the day as in the night. They, too, are exiles—perhaps not from you, but from freedom and dignity—and they hunger and thirst after equality and justice. They, too, long for deliverance. Make us conscious not only of your desire to satisfy that longing, but of our responsibility for its fulfillment. If they bear their suffering alone, make us aware of our guilt. If we greet their protest in silence, convict us of our cowardice. If we tolerate the boast of their oppressors, shatter our assumption of innocence. Empower us to be faithful to you, O Lord, and we shall be faithful to them.

Let the love that lifted Jesus' first disciples lift us. Raise our vision to the mountaintops, enabling us to scale the heights and leave behind the land and life of our exile forever.

❧ *Fifth Sunday in Lent.* O Lord, by whose grace slaves were set free and no people became your people, we too have felt your slave-liberating, people-making power. We worship you not only for the gracious past our ancestors shaped for us; we worship you also for the glorious future we are shaping for our descendants. We come unto you because you first came unto us; we seek you because you first sought us; and we love you because you first loved us. We are not your people because we chose you to be our God. We are your people because you chose us to be your people, and for this we give thanks.

But like the covenant-breakers of old, we have confused the roles of the Chooser and the chosen. You gave us a pen to write your law upon our hearts, but *our* voice guided the hand as it wrote. The law we inscribed there was all too often not yours but ours. You intended it as an instrument of liberation, but we have fashioned it into a tool of legalism. We no longer lay our animals on the altar of sacrifice, but neither do we lay ourselves on the altar of service. We no longer offend you with our presentation of burnt offerings, but neither do we please you with our presentation of contrite hearts. Forgive us, O God, for our mindless repetition of the folly of our ancestors, and renew with us the promise you made to them, for the sake of *our* descendants. Forgive our iniquity, and remember our sin no more, that we may know you as you know us and love our neighbors as you love them. Create in us a new heart, that we might break the old habits that estranged us. Deliver us from attachment to the land of our exile, that we might never again feel at home except in your presence.

We study the Gospel lesson with a mixture of joy and guilt. We are delighted that sometimes strangers still come to us, saying, "We would know Jesus." At the same time, we reproach ourselves that it happens so rarely. In ways unknown to us and in ways too well known to us, we have hidden him from view. We have contradicted our witness, invalidated our testimony, and betrayed our mission.

We pray, O Lord, for ourselves as individuals and for the church as a people, that your spirit will descend upon us and remake us from the inside out. Lift the scales from our eyes so that, when we look upon a world inhabited by diverse races and cultures, we shall behold the members of your family and ours. Render our hearts of stone into hearts of flesh so that, when we look at pictures of starving children, we shall behold the objects of your compassion and ours. And heal the paralysis of our limbs so that, when we look at the victims of injustice, we shall behold the beneficiaries of your redemption and ours. Christ has been lifted up; let him draw all people unto you, O God. So incline our hearts unto you that we shall hasten this global reunion of your people.

❧ *Passion/Palm Sunday.*   O God, who in Jesus became a member of our family that we might become members of your family, your grace astounds and confounds us. We stand amazed at the cost of our redemption. You turned away from no one, yet all turned away from you. You came to the members of your own household, but they greeted you as a stranger. You came to the members of your own synagogue, but they treated you as an alien. You came to the leaders of your own religion, but they dismissed you as a blasphemer. You came to the inner circle of your own disciples, but they forsook you as a loser. You came before the governor, and he offered you as a scapegoat.

Many of us have been tested, but our response has not been the same. Watching you, we can only echo the exclamation of the centurion, "Truly you are the Son of God." So today, like your disciples on that first Palm Sunday, we spread our branches and garments before you. In this way we glorify you, O Christ, not merely for the fact of your revelation of God, but for the manner of that revelation. By demonstrating the possibility of our union with God, you imply that we are responsible for our separation from God. Nevertheless, we are encouraged. Not only are we heartened by the assurance that our dreams and our deeds can become one. We are also reassured that the power of God will make them one.

As we relate the story of Jesus' entry into Jerusalem, we are confronted by the revelation not only of you but of us. We see you in the actions of Christ; ourselves, in the actions of those who turned his triumph into tragedy. The maneuvering of the chief priests and scribes, the avarice of Judas, the noisy boast of Peter, the drowsiness of the inner circle, the cry of the rabble, the mockery of the soldiers, the taunts of the passersby: This catalog of sins is all but endless and all too familiar. We have experienced many of them, firsthand.

Lord, we may not have been there when they crucified you then, but we are here when they crucify you now. Forgive us for siding with the crucifiers against the Crucified. And restore to us the joy of our salvation, that we may carry the cross with as much fervor as we sing about it.

There are many people for whom we should intercede, but we especially single out the victims of our faithless witness: those who look to us for generosity, but are repelled by our greed; those who look to us for boldness, but are put off by our hesitation; those who look to us for forthrightness, but are muted by our silence; those who look to us for compassion, but are stunned by our indifference; those who look to us for constancy, but are startled by our fickleness.

Deliver us, O Lord, from the weakness with which we have victimized those who have turned to us for strength. And fill us with your spirit, so that, when we stumble, they will not fall. Help them stand because they follow not our example but yours—the example of the one who set his face steadfastly toward Jerusalem,[8] even though he knew it would bring rejection and suffering.

❧ *Holy Thursday.*   Holy Thursday reminds us of the power and the peril of friendship. Despite the beauty of Jesus' love for the Twelve,

---

8. See Luke 9:51.

there came the tragedy of their betrayal. Yet, even after his disciples had forsaken him, he was not alone. You were there—as comforter, friend, and guide—to hear his cry of distress, to assure him of your presence, and to receive his spirit.

We adore you, dear Lord, for standing by him in his hour of trial and for standing by us in ours. No matter how fierce our foes or how fickle our friends, you are with us. So we thank you, dear Lord, for *your* friendship—a friendship that, even at our best, we could never deserve, and that, even at our worst, we could never destroy.

We wish, O Lord, that we could say that we have learned from the mistakes of the first disciples. But, as we review the crimes committed by the Twelve against Jesus, we are pressed to name a single one for which we could not also be indicted. They failed to make promises that they should have made, and they failed to keep some of the promises that they did make. Let us rebuke them if we dare, but let us not forget *our* promises, unmade and unkept. The Twelve, despite personal instruction by Jesus, never really understood him: Despite his warning that his mission was certain to attract enemies, they fled once those enemies showed their hand; after pledging to follow him to the death, they denied having known him and left him, friendless, before his accusers. Let us rebuke them if we dare, but let us not forget *our* transgressions, witting and unwitting.

It is not the Twelve or the Seventy or even our brothers and our sisters who stand most in need of prayer. It is we—we who have misunderstood and betrayed and deserted you, we who have left you alone to face your enemies and ours. Wherefore, dear Lord, we ask not only for your forgiveness, but for the renewal of your spirit in us.

As we partake together of the one cup and the one loaf, let us be reminded that they attest to our unity—our unity with friends like ourselves, weak, rebellious, and fickle; and our unity with you, O Lord, the friend who counters weakness with strength, rebellion with obedience, and fickleness with faithfulness. Let our communion be more than a participation in your death. Let it also be an extension of your life.

❧ *Good Friday.* O God, in Jesus you became subject to us that we might become subject to you. Your reconciling presence was at work in his ministry, and not merely when he was in control, healing and teaching and preaching. It was no less at work in him when others were in control, betraying, mocking, and crucifying him. This we firmly believe. We are witnesses to the gospel that you were in Jesus reconciling the world, not only after the resurrection and Pentecost, but in his rejection and suffering and death.

We thank you, O God, for revealing in him the mind you intend for us all, proclaiming through your incarnation in him the possibility of your incarnation in us. It is no more blasphemous to say we can be like him than to say he was like you. He was the Son of man *and* the Son of God; Jesus of earth and Christ of heaven. And he was the prophet who declared, "You shall do greater works than these."[9]

Yet we have been slow to follow the example of our Servant Lord in suffering for the sins of others. Worse yet, we have denied responsibility for our own sins. And we have excused ourselves by blaming our troubled times. We should have thought, instead, of the troubled times of Jesus, and how that he, when friends forsook him, appealed his case to a higher court; how that he, when even that appeal brought no justice, was faithful unto death; and how that he, in death as in life, showed the way to you.

O God, when our neighbors come to us in search of direction, help us point them beyond their weakness to your greatness, that you might do for them through us what you have done for us through others.

---

9. See John 14:12.

Easter Season

❋ *Easter.*　Almighty God, who set the sun in the heavens to light up the earth by day and the moon and the stars by night, you sent Jesus Christ to earth to light up our life by day and by night. We celebrate your gift of life. As you chased the shadows of the deep, you have shattered the darkness of Calvary. Now we know that nothing can ever again separate us from the light with which you flood all creation in Jesus Christ.

O light of the world, on Easter you dug the grave of darkness. Today we commemorate your victory, not only of light over darkness and life over death, but of love over hate and meaning over mystery. We thank you for Easter's reversal of Good Friday. We had heard of your judgments by the mouths of the prophets, but now we have confirmation of them from the Lord of life: that you judge not by what the eyes see and the ears hear but by what justice requires and truth demands; that you judge not with favor for the mighty but with equity for the meek; that you decide not with rewards for oppressors but with amends for the oppressed.

Yet our acts of pride compromise our words of praise. We more often echo the prophets' pronouncements of divine judgment with our lips than with our lives. Our love does not render us blind to the sights or deaf to the sounds of selfish ambition. Our love does not check our preference for the company of the mighty over the meek. Our love does not move us to champion the cause of the oppressed against oppressors. We call ourselves your Easter people, but we daily resurrect the life that Jesus crucified.

We are not what you would have us be. Yet we long to become what you would have us become. So we pray, O Lord, not only for the forgiveness of our deafness and blindness and silence, but we pray also for your renewal of our hearing and sight and speech. Open our ears to the cries of the deprived and the depraved, lest our deafness continue to aggravate the misery of the miserable. Open our eyes to the plight of the sick and hungry, lest our blindness compound the neglect of the neglected. Loose our tongues to proclaim the promise of life, lest Easter be reduced to a memory of the past without meaning for the present.

O risen Christ, who joined a company of your disciples on the Emmaus road, we are grateful that your walk among us did not end in Emmaus; that, even now, you go before us to show us the way to your mission and ours. We can do all things through you who strengthens us.

You break down the middle wall of partition, that you might reconcile us to God in one body. Empower us, dear Lord, to become faithful witnesses to your wall-breaking gospel of reconciliation. Do it, we beseech you, not in spite of us but through us. Make us one in our witness to the triumph of Easter, that we might become one in our witness to the God of Easter.

O Light of the world, illumine our hearts, that we might feel your compassion; illumine our minds, that we might discern your will; and illumine our path, that we might carry your mission to the ends of the earth, through Jesus Christ our Lord.

❦ *Second Sunday of Easter.* O God, who in Jesus sent your life to earth and on Easter revealed your power over death, we bless you in the name of Christ our Lord. We cannot know the risen Christ as Thomas demanded to know him. We cannot touch the print of the nails in his hands or gaze at the wounds in his side. But we can know him in the power of his resurrection. Jesus left us, but he did not leave us alone. Before taking his leave of earth, he breathed your spirit on his disciples, enabling them to recall his words and deeds and to interpret them. That same spirit is still at work. Not only does it enable Christ to become our contemporary; it enables us to become contemporary with Christ. We do not have to envy those first disciples. For just as Christ became their companion on the Emmaus road, he becomes our companion on the roads we travel. As he walked with them, he walks with us. And if we will but listen, he will also talk with us. Moreover, if we will walk in his steps, he will claim us as his own.

O Lord of heaven and earth, who was never more truly present with us than when you joined humankind in Christ, we adore you for revealing yourself in Jesus, as you were and are and evermore shall be. As we thank you for him, we thank you also for those who have kept his spirit alive. Their name may not be Legion, but their presence is undeniable. As he gave himself to your mission, they give themselves to his mission. As he bore witness to the unity between God and humankind, they bear witness to the unity between Christ and the church.

Yet our life as a Christian community has rarely moved outsiders to exclaim that we are one with Jesus. Unlike those who did evoke this testimony, we are not of one mind and one spirit. We betray our claim to unity with you by our practice of divisions among ourselves.

Forgive us, dear Lord, for this betrayal of those who come to us in search of bread for the journey. We cannot but feel guilty that our love has not been more generous: that oppressors have looked to us for silence, and not in vain; that the victims of the system have looked to us for justice, but in vain.

As we intercede in prayer for these victims of our faithlessness, send us forth to put life into our words. Restore their faith in you through our demonstration of faith in them. Awaken us to your will, that we may awaken them to your will. Renew your partnership with us so that your spirit will infuse our partnership with them. And let us and them, hand in hand with you and one another, go into the world to perform the mission to which Christ has commissioned us. Let us not forget that, in faith as in life, we all rely on mentors. Grant us the grace, dear Lord, so to represent you that we will neither displease you nor mislead others.

❧ *Third Sunday of Easter.* O God, who in Jesus revealed the love that endows life with significance, the purpose that gives direction to humanity, and the power that spells death for evil, you are our Lord and a great God above all gods. We worship you, for your revelation in Jesus will not permit us to offer you anything less than our worship.

For this manifestation of your grace, we thank you, dear Lord. From this storehouse of riches we have continually drawn, yet the treasury has not been depleted. For like all the spiritual capital with which you have entrusted us, it is something we can lose only by failing to use it. This truth you have written deep into the heart of us all. We thank you, gracious Lord, for thus ordering our existence. Not only does it mean that we can find purpose for our life. It also demands that we respect the lives of others.

Yet we cannot ponder your gift without asking forgiveness for its abuse. We may be quick to hail the power of Jesus' name, but we are slow to spread our trophies at his feet: We are as apt to expect him to crown us as we are to crown him. He has opened our minds that we may understand the Scriptures, but we have hardened our hearts against his interpretation of them. He has enacted the role of the Lord's suffering servant, but our faith becomes skeptical when "bad" things happen to "good" people. We sing that there is a cross for everyone, but we wait for Jesus to carry not only his but ours.

Paul proclaimed "Christ and him crucified," but we proclaim a gospel of ecstasy without agony. Whereas for Jesus Calvary was a way of life, we have turned it into a way of death. And whereas Easter marked your stamp of approval on Jesus' way of life, we have reduced the resurrection to a proof of the immortality of the soul. Forgive us, O God, for thus mocking the meaning and message of our Lord Jesus Christ.

We pray, O Lord, that you will so rule our hearts that we will make you known not only in the breaking of the bread but in the sharing of the bread: that we shall shoulder the cross you carried for the poor and oppressed; that we shall recognize that repentance, like charity, must begin at home; that we shall accept the forgiveness of Christ, not merely as a revelation of the divine character, but as a model for human behavior; and that we shall bring into being the fellowship of kindred minds for which Jesus prayed.

O God, let us not lose sight of the connection between Easter and Good Friday. Let us remember that, if Easter demonstrates your ability to work the divine will without our help, Good Friday confirms that your victories do not come without cost to us. Deliver us from the lure of cheap grace. Make us as willing to pay the cost of your victories as we are to claim them for ourselves.

❧ *Fourth Sunday of Easter.*   O God, our Creator, when we consider humanity, we marvel at our endless variety. You have measured us with different yardsticks; some of us are small, others large. You have painted us with different brush strokes; we belong to diverse races. You have endowed us with different talents; some of us work with our hands, others with our minds. You have crowned us with glory and honor; you have put within our reach a marvelous harmony of sight and sound and sense. You have so made us that, apart from such harmony, we cannot experience the abundant life that you intend; that, if we would live the abundant life, we must acknowledge our dependence upon one another and upon you. To realize your purpose for us, we must so learn to care for one another that, when one of us suffers, we all suffer, and that, when one of us rejoices, we all rejoice.

Yet we have frustrated your purpose and turned your harmony into discord. We treasure the Scriptures that celebrate the quest for unity in diversity, yet we look with contempt on interpretations that depart from our own. We acknowledge you to be the Good Shepherd of the sheep of other folds, yet we foment conflict with the sheep of our own fold. Worse yet, we claim divine sanction for these divisions of our own making. And we proceed to justify our little love for one another by appeal to our devotion to Jesus Christ.

Forgive us, O God, not only for the ease with which we break communion with our brothers and sisters, but for the arrogance with which we lay the credit at your door. Save us from usurping your role as Judge, lest we be judged by the judgment with which we judge others.[10] Give us hearts that are generous as well as penitent: penitent, for we know how you deplore our pulling apart; and generous, for we know how you applaud our pulling together. We pray for the grace to strive for the unity of your fold. Bring us together in one flock, O God, that you may be the Good Shepherd of us all.

❧ *Fifth Sunday of Easter.*   O God, in the beginning you created heaven and earth. And, one day, as you walked upon the land, you came upon a very fertile hill and imagined there a vineyard purple with grapes. So with your own hands you dug it and cleared it of stones, and planted it with choice vines; long you tended it and looked for it to yield its fruit, but it yielded only wild grapes.[11]

No more could you have done for your vineyard, Lord. Your pleasant planting turned bitter and rebelled against you. You looked for justice, but, behold, we bore bloodshed; you looked for righteousness, but, behold, we produced a cry!

You could have become angry, Lord. You could have removed the hedge that protected the yard, that we might be devoured by the beasts. You could have broken down its wall, that we might be trampled. You could have laid it waste, and let our briers and thorns grow up; you could have commanded the clouds to withhold their rains, so that nothing would grow.

But even as you are our Creator and Sustainer, O God, you are our Redeemer. And you planted again in our midst. You set out at the center of the vineyard the true vine. And the vine has grown; it cannot be destroyed, it cannot bear bad fruit. Its good fruit hangs heavy on the branches, bearing witness to your care.

Christ is the vine, Lord; make us the branches. Whatever you ask us to be, we shall be; whatever you ask us to do, shall be done.

This truth amazes us, that you sent the true vine to save us not because we first loved you, but because you first and last loved us. By this we are humbled, Lord, for you are Alpha and Omega, Beginning

---

10. See Matthew 7:2.
11. This and the following imagery is drawn from Isaiah 5.

and End, Love that began the beginning and knows no end. Yours is the love that birthed the world and makes it grow. It is the love that grasped Philip as he preached and drove him to carry the news of his new faith beyond the bounds of Judaism—even to places his old faith had considered unclean. It is the love that grasped the mighty Ethiopian as he sat in his chariot and drove him with a new faith into the waters of his baptism—to a new life his old life had never imagined.

Yours is the love, Lord, that changes the world, inside and out. The ones unclean in the world's eyes, your love makes clean. The ones mighty in the world's eyes, your love makes humble. The ones guilty in the world's eyes, your love ushers into paradise.

Lord, for this we praise you, that you first and last love us. Now what remains is for you to teach us how better to love one another. Teach us, Lord, the truth of life, before the hour is late; lead us, Lord, in the way we should go, before the gate is closed.

Bring us now into your vineyard, Lord. Prune us and tend us, that we may bear good fruit. We offer you all that we are; press us into the wine of the new covenant, that the cup of the new kingdom may be filled to overflowing.

❧ *Sixth Sunday of Easter.* O Lord, your first group of followers was a motley lot. Fishermen, housewives, tax collectors, prostitutes, rebels, and more: Some of them would have been mutual enemies had Christ not brought them together, and most would have walked through their lives indifferent to one another, for each had traveled a different road, and each had harbored different hopes. And yet in Christ their crowded ways crossed. Their lives intersected for all time. Now they were promised that the way of one would become the way of many, that the hope of one would become the hope of many.

O Lord, we are just as motley a lot. Some of us have had our differences, and many of us have been indifferent. We have traveled our own roads and harbored our own fears. And yet, in Christ, our crowded ways have crossed, intersecting for all time. And Christ has become for us, as for the first disciples, our way and our hope.

As your people, God, we are given a new identity. We become your servants, and we serve with gladness. But this is not all. You sent Christ among us with a new word, that we are *more* than servants. "No longer do I call you servants," he declared, "for the servant does not know what the master is doing; but I have called you friends, for all that I have heard from God, I have made known to you. You did not choose me, but I chose you."

Your child, Jesus Christ, *chooses* us, not as mere servants, but as friends; chooses us to know what we had never known before, to do what we had never done before, to be what we had never been before. He chooses us, not because we are worthy to be chosen, but because he serves the unworthy. He chooses us, not because we have been washed free of sin, but because he washes the feet of sinners. He chooses us, not because of our performance in the past, but because of his faith in our future.

He chooses us to be his friends. He makes us his equals, instilling in us the capacity for compassion, inspiring in us the spirit of understanding, and arousing in us the desire for action. He chooses us, saying, "Truly, truly, they who believe in me will also do the works that I do; and greater works than these will they do." [12]

This, then, is our new identity: Though we be the servants of God, we are the friends of Christ. This, then, is our new calling: to love one another even as we have been loved. This, then, is our new commandment: that we love our God with all our being, and our neighbors as ourselves. This, then, is our new life: for they who love are born of God. This, then, is our new faith: that they who are born of God have the victory. Through Christ we are the victors over differences, and over indifference. Through Christ we are victors over the world that crucifies its God! Through Christ we are victors over the grave!

❦ *Seventh Sunday of Easter.*

O God, you sent a fragile, strong life into a strong, fragile world. That life grew, and he was called the Lord of the Dance. But the world frowned upon the dance he danced and nailed his feet to a tree. That life grew, and he was called the Singer of the Song. But the world grimaced at the song he sang, and lifted vinegar to his lips. That life grew, and he was called the Ruler of Life. But the world scorned the life he lived and gambled away his purple robe.

O God, you sent a fragile, strong life. A screaming baby, he was wrapped in swaddling cloths and laid in a manger. A silent body, he was wrapped in linen cloths and laid in a tomb. He was like us, one day thrust into the world, one day thrust from it. The challenges that lay

---

12. See John 14:12.

between his manger and his tomb were different from ours, but his mission was the same: to awaken to the knowledge that we are one with you; to awaken to the knowledge that we are brothers and sisters and you, our father and mother; to awaken to the knowledge that, in you and in one another, we shall find birth, life, and rebirth.

Just as the cloths in our manger are replaced by child's clothes, the shrouds in the tomb are not our final garments. In you we have life: a fragile yet strong life; a life capable of bearing the cross, confident that the cross will not have the last word; a life trembling as it enters the tomb, trusting that it will rise again; a life crucified, dead, buried, and resurrected on the third day, day after day after day.

In you, O God, we have life, not for our own sake, but for the sake of this world. As you sent Christ into the world to save it, so you send us. Strengthen our fragility, Lord, that we may not break. Weaken our strength, Lord, that we may not burst. For self-contempt and self-pride are the dragons on our daily road between manger and tomb, death and return.

Lord, tend our life that it may grow. And, if the world sees in us the Lord of the Dance, let it put away its hammer and nails and leap with us. If the world hears in us the Singer of the Song, let it spill its vinegar upon the ground and join our chorus. If the world feels in us the Ruler of Life, let it cast its dice into the sea and take with us the risk of faith.

For the sake of our world, O God, we dedicate our feet, our lips, and our lives, that our world may be consecrated in truth and baptized in life.

Season After Pentecost

❧ _Pentecost._ O wise and gracious God, how intimately you know the creation that your hand is fashioning, that breathes the wind of your spirit!

Though you have an infinite ability to preserve, you have so designed creation that resurrection, not preservation, is the aim of all life. You have set the seasons turning in their cycle; you have set the earth spinning, circling the sun like an immortal lover.

All is change, all is motion: This is your will, that even in the endless red heat of the Sahara the sands will creep before the wind, and even over the endless blue ice of the Arctic the sun will sink before the stars. Since the beginning, evening has followed morning, and you have declared the day good.

This is the way of this world, for in the soil of your hand eternity is a flower, and in the ocean of your eye immortality is the tide. This you know, but we desire not change but permanence; not motion but repose; not evening and morning but eternal noon. We would use our freedom to protect what we have at this moment and to perpetuate who we are at this time.

O wise and gracious God, you create us in your image, but we hide it well. Your messenger, Jesus Christ, worked to awaken us to the holy temple within us, where the change and motion of death and resurrection receive your blessing. He died and arose as its crowning expression. But, predictably, when he had risen, we had difficulty recognizing him, because he was no longer the same. We would not believe, because he was different. When he was dead, we had wanted him back, we had longed for "the good old days." But his return brought a new day, and he was not back to stay.

We begged him not to go. But he replied that it was to our advantage that he leave; if he did not, the Spirit would not come. He knew that, if he remained, we would _use_ him. He had walked his road; we would bronze his steps. He had preached the gospel; we would engrave it in stone. He had carried his cross; we would adore it as a relic. He had conquered the grave; we would kneel at the tomb. Jesus knew that, if he remained, he would forever be merely the focus of our wonder and the object of our worship—our excuse for looking to a past already gone instead of a future yet to come. We would preserve him instead of serving him. Eternal noon would be confined to Sunday morning. We would commit him to the tomb once again, and thereby banish our lives to the same fate.

Your messenger knew this, and so, despite our protests, he left us, that we might dwell in your Spirit—the spirit of wisdom and understanding, the spirit of counsel and might, the spirit of knowledge and awe;[13] the spirit that moved over the face of the waters in the beginning of time.[14]

O God, in our hands you have placed the seeds of the eternal flower. In the power of your Spirit, let us not hold them forever, but risk their planting. In our eyes you have placed droplets of the immortal tide. In the power of your Spirit, let us not keep them forever, but risk their running. For through the planting of the seed shall your kingdom grow, through the crying of the tear shall your seed flourish, and through dying and rising shall your people live.

✤ *Trinity Sunday (First Sunday After Pentecost).* O One who is as no other, we dare to call upon your name, for you have revealed that we, like Christ, are one with you.[15] In you our bodies dwell; in you our spirits breathe; in you our minds explore. In you our births are begun, and our deaths, transformed. In you our hopes reside, and our fears are harbored.

We celebrate this, our oneness with you: As your daughters, we rise up; as your sons, we grow; as sisters and brothers of Christ, we discover our power and our vulnerability. But we must also confess that we have often celebrated this mysterious union while casting an uncertain glance over our shoulder.

Like Isaiah, we welcome your call—as long as you call us to pleasantries. Like Nicodemus, we seek your answers—as long as they conform to common logic. Like your earliest disciples, we hail every sign of your presence—as long as it satisfies our expectations.

So you see, Lord, while you say that we are one with you, we are not convinced. We are only willing to offer you *parts* of ourselves. You want us to jump in with both feet? We will put one foot in and keep one foot out. You want us to be single-minded? We will split every hair of every argument. You want us to commit our spirits? We will divide ourselves right down the middle, like the baby of Solomon's legend. You can have half, we say, and that will have to do.

But that does *not* do, does it? Even the most imaginative mathemati-

---

13. Inspired by Isaiah 11:2.
14. See Genesis 1:2.
15. See John 17:11.

cian cannot cut oneness in two and still have one. Oneness simply *is*. We have no choice in the matter. It is not that you *prefer* us to *become* one with you; in Christ you have *demonstrated* that we *are* one with you.

Are we too afraid to confess it, too stubborn to acknowledge it? Whatever the reason, we have shrunk from the truth, hiding in any corner of life that we could find, thinking that there you could not find us. But always you are there, because that is where *we* are.

"Truly, truly . . . unless one is born anew, one cannot see the kingdom of God." We must begin all over again, Lord. Teach us again how to see, but this time through *your* eyes. Teach us again to walk, this time in *your* shoes. Teach us again to feel, this time through *your* senses. Teach us again to love, this time with *your* heart.

O One, who is as no other yet one with all, help us to be born again. Inspire in us the confidence that you will be born with us, that you will grow with us. Then we shall surely perceive the kingdom where, before, we perceived only dust—in the world and in ourselves.

❦ *Sunday Between May 29 and June 4 (if After Trinity Sunday).* Almighty God, what power you pour out upon us! What possibilities you instill within us! You fill our hearts, these fragile earthen pots, with strength and promise. A treasure, indeed, you bestow.

Yet we are tempted to hide it, to hoard it. While we conserve our power for some rainy day, the powerless are consumed around us. While we preserve our potential for the day of destiny, the actual threatens us with the day of doom.

It is an old story, Lord, heard and told a hundred times. Yet we have not learned. We must still confess our resemblance to Eli, the cowardly chief priest of Israel, who knew of his sons' abuse of their priestly office but whose love of his position made him reluctant to discipline them. Like him, we rely less on your power than on our judgment. Our concern is less for your purpose than for our privilege.

We must also acknowledge our likeness to the Pharisees, whose authority was bound by a rigid religion. Like them, we depend less on your mercy than on our purity. Our loyalty is less to our neighbors than to our rules.

Remind us, O God, that Jesus Christ our Lord was a rule-breaker; that he called tax collectors as disciples, partied with sinners, and even healed people on the sabbath. Teach us that sometimes, like him, we may have to break human rules in fidelity to a higher law—the law of love. Remind us, too, that Jesus Christ stood against all authorities to proclaim that law, even unto death on a cross. Remind us lest we, like the Pharisees, should plot against truth; lest we, like Eli, should dishonor our calling.

Your purpose, O God, will not be thwarted. You have poured out your power upon us! You have instilled your possibilities within us! You have filled our hearts, these fragile earthen pots, with strength and promise. If some of us become misers and hoard the treasure you have placed within us, open the generous hearts of others and loose their treasures upon the earth. In the redemption of the world, let their treasures be returned to you a thousandfold.

✤ *Sunday Between June 5 and June 11 (if After Trinity Sunday).* O God, hear our prayer! We need to know that, beyond us, you are. For while we seek our own salvation, it cannot be had through striving. We think highly of ourselves, O Lord, but we are not great—only driven by dreams of greatness. And we have stumbled upon such dreams until finally we have fallen and plunged into the pit.

We cannot see; the midnight-dark steals our sight. We cannot breathe; the stale air smothers our breath. We cannot hear; our pounding heart deafens our ears. We cannot bear it. For here, in the pit, we meet our demons, our fiercest enemies, our terrible idols—things seen substituted for things unseen; things fleeting worshiped in place of things eternal. Here, in the pit, the fact of our baseness explodes the myth of our greatness. Here, in the pit, we stand alone.

And yet, O God, we are not alone. For suddenly we perceive that we are cowering in the midst of lions. These are the royal powers upon which we may call—powers you have set within us to prey upon the demons and consume the false gods. Give us courage in their presence; let us trust them. By devouring all within us that is not yours, they shall carry us up and out of the pit.

Yes, Lord, we shall be saved! Reveal to us our potential for evil and for good, that the pit might become the crest of your mountain, and our fall, a fall upward to you!

✤ *Sunday Between June 12 and June 18 (if After Trinity Sunday).* Awakener of dreams and Revealer of visions, reveal yourself to our hibernating spirits and awaken us from our sleep. Long have we snuggled in secret places, shut off from any new sign of spring. Long have we slumbered through the winters of the soul, wrapped in an apathy that seeks only to be forgotten; frozen in an indifference that seeks only to be sheltered.

This is the eternal winter that chills our nerve and hardens our heart. Our memory of spring soon fades, and we cease expecting her approach. We no longer await the thaw of the earth, the warmth of the sun, or the bud of the flower, for there is nothing for which to hope. We become those who walk by sight, not by faith; and because the sight of deepest winter is not pleasing to our eyes, we soon do not walk at all.

O Lord, arouse in our dormant hearts a vision of the springtime, when the old has passed away and the new has come; when the bitter cold has fled before the sun, and the whipping wind has died before a breeze, and the forgotten flower has opened in morning dew. For while the world sleeps, the silent sower sows the seeds, and no frost nips their blossoms. These are the mysterious seeds of the kingdom, yielding the flower of faith and the blossom of righteousness.

Awaken us, O God, to this sweet scent that plays at the nostril. This rich, upturned earth awaits its planting; plant your seeds, and we shall tend them. Scatter your seeds, and we shall baptize them. Tuck them into good soil, and we shall pluck the weeds. Multiply them, and we shall harvest. The bounty of that harvest shall be your joy, and its plenty shall be our hope. For as the seasons of the field change, so too the seasons of the heart; and where once there was winter, now there is spring.

❦ *Sunday Between June 19 and June 25 (if After Trinity Sunday).*   O God, yours is the work of creation, of inspiration, of striking a spark in the darkness, of carving a figure from stone. Yours is the work of transformation, of change, of luring a spring from winter, of coaxing a day from night. Yours is the work of reconciliation, of union, of bonding humanity and nature, of joining human to human.

You reveal yourself to us as the One who creates, transforms, and reconciles, and for no small purpose. In so doing, you reveal to us: ourselves. Made in your image, ours too is revealed to be the work of creation, transformation, and reconciliation.

No small responsibility. You have placed in our hands our own generation, and the next and the next as well. Perhaps in the ancient world it was enough for one of your servants to ask, "Am I my brother's keeper?" But that question today is dwarfed by our world. Today not only the brother, but the sister; not only the sister, but the friend; not only the friend, but the enemy; not only the enemy, but the unnamed; not only the unnamed, but the unborn; not only the unborn, but the unforeseen—all generations of peoples, creatures, and worlds are in our hands. And somehow, in your great hope and even greater mercy, you can acknowledge this and still say to us, "Behold, I see what I have made, and it is good."

O Lord, we fear that our hands shall tremble; we are terrified by the task you have given us. We are poor caretakers of this world. We have ravaged our lands, and still we plunder; we have defiled our seas, and still we pollute; we have poisoned our air, and still we discharge. And now we are shuttling off into space, toward unknown worlds, as if we were fleeing from our own destruction.

O God, if we are to be creators, give us the drive to create life, rather than death. If we are to be transformers, give us the power to transform the ugly into the beautiful, rather than the beautiful into the ugly. If we are to be reconcilers, give us the compassion to reconcile for peace and justice, rather than for truce and power. If, O God, we are to do your work in the midst of and on behalf of our brother and our sister, our friend and our enemy, the unnamed and the unborn and the unforeseen, we can do so only because of who *you* are, and who we can become through faith in you.

❦ _Sunday Between June 26 and July 2._ O God, we look to you this day for signs of your presence. We do not doubt that you are here, for there is no place where you are not. We doubt, rather, that your presence can alter the circumstances of our present. You are unseen, but our loyalty is to the seen. We trust things more than we trust people; we have more faith in people than we have in you. For things and people are familiar, and noticeable, while the movements of your Spirit are strange and subtle. Things and people—we believe that we can control them; but your Spirit—it blows where it wills, and we do not know whence it comes or whither it goes.[16]

And so, O God, we request a sign, some simple epiphany. We do not

---

16. See John 3:8.

demand it, for we stand on holy ground; our feet are bare and unclean, and no hands but yours can wash them.

We are not alone in our request. The Israelites built the ark of the covenant, wherein your Spirit might dwell. They *knew* that your presence filled its space; they believed so absolutely, we are told, that whoever brushed against its gilded wood—the house of the living God—fell dead. The ark was *their* sign, but it was of their making, and carried with it life and death.

The crowds demanded signs of Jesus. But they scoffed when the wonders were not great enough; they envied when the wonders were too great; they threatened when the wonders appeared in the wrong place or at the wrong time or to the wrong people. Healings were *their* signs—a crippled hand made straight, a blind eye made seeing—but the signs had to be of *their* design; and thus, their demands carried with them less life than death.

And the death of the healer was their ultimate demand. The death of your supreme sign, O God; we clamored for his crucifixion. O Lord, we want your sign, but you know that on one day we shall celebrate it, and on the next, we shall kill it. If you send us prophets, we shall slander them, stone them, shoot them, crucify them. If you send us liberators, we shall blame them, betray them, break them, and bury them. If you send us signs, O Lord, we shall ignore them or imitate them or injure them or idolize them—but we shall not receive them as you receive us.

Dear God, we cannot request a sign. But request it we must, for little is our faith. Appear among us, and unveil our eyes that we might see you. Speak to us, and unstop our ears that we might hear you. Enlighten us, and illumine our minds that we might understand you. Embrace us, and open our hearts that we might care—before it is too late. Through our little faith in that which is seen and heard and understood and felt, we shall find the fullness of faith in you.

✤ <u>*Sunday Between July 3 and July 9.*</u>   O God of all, we rest in the knowledge that wherever we are, there shall you be also. Whether we reside in the palace of a king or the house of a carpenter; the mansion of a president or the dwelling of a tenant: ours is your dwelling-place. Whether we labor in the seat of a government or the assembly line of a factory; in the classroom of a school or the ward of a hospital: ours is your workplace. And even if our home be the street, and the door of the workplace be barred, ours is your resting place.

You are with us always, for yours is a loyalty that surpasses the greatest love we have ever known. It is a loyalty that persists through all terrors; survives, despite all betrayals; and endures, for all generations. Greater love has no one than this: You have laid down your love for the life of the world.

Let this loyalty of yours—so unknown, so strange—arouse in us a commitment to envision more, to do more, to be more. And not "more" only, but more *for you*. Give us the courage to surrender to you our weakness, that you might make it our strength. Grant us the humility to yield to you our power, that you might fill it with grace. And endow us with the confidence to submit to you our will, that you might adapt it to your purpose.

Our commitment to you shall render us unknown, shall make us strangers among many who once knew us. They will remember us in old roles, with old habits and haunts. The more we envision the kingdom, the more they will call us back to the "real" world. The more we do the work of the kingdom, the more their eyebrows will wrinkle. The more we *are* the kingdom, the more they will long for the persons we once were.

O God of all, we rest in the knowledge that wherever we are, there shall you be also. But that place where we dwell together—the kingdom of heaven on earth—is not an easy place in which to dwell. Help us to understand that our identity and mission must not depend on the acceptance of those who do not understand; that its success or failure must never be measured in human terms.

❧ *Sunday Between July 10 and July 16.*   O God, you have created us for yourself and for one another in a world of your own making. You are Lord above all lords and God above all gods; and you are our Lord and our God. You are the light unto our path; were it not for you, we would dwell in deep darkness. You are the strength of our life; were it not for you, we could not resist the powers of evil. You are the hope of our tomorrows; were it not for you, we would break under the load of our yesterdays.

As we bow before you, dear Lord, refresh our memories. Let us not forget where we are, whose we are, or what the reason for our gifts. Remind us that the land in which we dwell, wherever it be, is your land; that the people among whom we dwell, whoever they be, are your people; and that the gifts with which we are endowed, whatever they be, are bestowed to make us one in our worship of you and our service to one another.

We have repeatedly affirmed these elementary truths of our faith. Yet we confess, O Lord, that only rarely have we made them the truths of our lives. We have treated the land as if we were not its stewards but its owners. We have dealt with other people as if our relationships were of no concern to you. And we have handled our gifts as if they were intended to set people apart rather than bring them together.

We thank you, dear Lord, for your gift of these precious truths of faith and for all those who have sought to teach us their importance. For our disregard of their teaching, we ask your forgiveness. And we pray that you will give us hearts so attuned to your will that we will proceed to do it.

Remind us of our responsibility toward those who look to us for guidance. Let us not greet this responsibility with excuses. Save us from the temptation to exaggerate our inadequacies and our obstacles. Let us dwell, instead, on your mighty acts wrought through people of equally unpromising circumstances—the slaves in Egypt, the harp player from Bethlehem, the Carpenter from Nazareth, the tentmaker from Tarsus. As we ponder the lives of those who shaped our faith, we see people who looked not within or around but up. They gave up the inward look, anxiously trying accurately to assess their strengths and weaknesses. They gave up the outward look, nervously trying to separate their friends from their foes. And they adopted the upward look, faithfully seeking to conform their will to yours.

O God, you have commanded us to do unto others what we would have them do unto us. Enable us to give unto others the greatest gift others have given us. Face to face with the tensions within, troubles without, and threats on every side, help us follow the example of those who turned neither inward nor outward but upward. When our neighbors ask us for guidance, let us introduce them to our Guide.

🍁 <u>*Sunday Between July 17 and July 23.*</u>   O God, your glory fills heaven and earth; your creation is greater than our powers to describe. We are your creatures; and you, our Creator. Who are we that you are mindful of us?[17] The distance between us could not be bridged from our side to yours; so you bridged it from your side to ours.

---

17. See Psalm 8:4.

Despite our disregard for you, our contempt for your law, and our violation of your covenant, in Jesus Christ you took upon yourself our human frame. In him you assumed all the limits and braved all the risks of every person born of earth. In him you became a member of our family that we might become members of your family. In him you turned our adoring eyes from the majesty of creation to the love of the Creator. For this, the mightiest of all your mighty acts, we worship you.

We thank you, dear Lord, that in Jesus you rejected our low opinion of human nature: for laying bare our preference for crowns over crosses; and for exposing our habit of sacrificing the joy of eternity for the pleasure of the moment. When we behold ourselves in him, we cannot but exclaim that you have made us little less than God and crowned us with glory and honor.[18]

But when we look away from him to ourselves, we behold a very different creature. We see a king shamelessly pursuing his ambition, ignoring the traditions of his people, to build a great temple. We discover that the enemy we most have to fear is the enemy within: that in our hearts there lurks a breaker of all those commandments designed to protect our neighbors from ourselves. The sight of this demon disgusts us, but we do not have to surrender to its power. Help us, dear Lord, so to fix our hearts upon Christ, that the good we *would,* we *do;* and the evil we would *not,* we *do not.*[19]

O God, our towns are full of people like the crowds that flocked to Jesus—sheep without a shepherd. Yet we know to which flock they belong, for we know who their shepherd is. Lead us to them, that we might lead them to you: that we and they might become one flock; that you might be the Good Shepherd of us all; and that, with singleness of mind and purity of heart, we might heed your voice.

❧ *Sunday Between July 24 and July 30.*   Eternal and gracious God, whose standards reflect your goodness and who does not wink at their disregard, we adore you for your character and integrity. We stand in awe of your righteousness and of your lofty expectations, but we would not have it otherwise. Nothing so reassures us as the knowledge that you, our maker, are also our judge; that, if your demands are high, it is because you know that we are capable of meeting them; that, when you send prophets among us for our correction, it

---

18. See Psalm 8:5.
19. See Romans 7:15-20.

is not to assert your authority but to preserve our humanity; and that, even when we treat you with disrespect, you continue to respect us. We thank you, dear Lord, not only for your faith in us, but for your faithfulness toward us. We thank you for raising up prophets to rebuke us for our evil deeds, even as the psalmist confronted Israel.

Yet we must confess that the prophets of our time do not fare much better than the prophets of antiquity. We may not kill them as did the ancients, but neither do we crown them with halos. We cry out for them boldly to declare the will of the Lord. However, as soon as they begin to express opinions contrary to our own, we begin to question their credentials. If they call for an end to the arms race, we accuse them of abandoning tough minds for tender hearts. If they call for an end to racism, we accuse them of replacing realism with idealism. If they call for applying the brakes to nationalism, we accuse them of trading history for utopia. If they call for a war on poverty, we accuse them of sacrificing ambition for equality. If they call for the rehabilitation of criminals, we accuse them of defending the villains instead of the victims.

Forgive us, O God, for our response to our prophets. We may sometimes be right in questioning their solutions, but we are not right in ignoring the problems to which they point. Their remedies may not always be the best, but the wrongs they address are real. So we repent, O God, for thinking and for acting as if we could get rid of our problems by discrediting those who call them to our attention: for fragmenting your family, and for neatly separating the sheep from the goats, the innocent from the guilty, and the villains from the victims.

Help us, O God, to realize that we live in a world much too dangerous for such uncharitable attitudes. Help us see that we cannot remake the world, save as you, through Christ, have remade us: by living for you, dying unto self, and loving the undeserving. Give us the will so to enflesh this vision that we will make the world safe for your prophets—ready to grant that, if you be for them, we dare not be against them.

✤ *Sunday Between July 31 and August 6.*   O God, you have created us to depend on one another; if we do not work together, we will tear the world apart. You have made us debtors to those who have gone before us; if we do not learn from them, we will cripple the world for those who will come after us. You have bestowed on us gifts to make us one; if we do not share them, we will not reach the better world toward which you would lead us. We praise you for entrusting us with so great a responsibility.

If only our faith were as great as your trust! But our record, at best, has been spotted. Instead of depending on others to work for the good of all, we have simply neglected them. Instead of learning from the experiences of previous generations, we have simply repeated them. Instead of distributing your gifts according to need, we have simply hoarded them.

For this betrayal of you, we ask your forgiveness, O God. Not only have we betrayed you as a people; we have betrayed you as individuals. Each of us has worked to delay the coming of your rule to earth. We know the power of lies to hurt, yet we have let gossip go unchecked. We know the power of silence to scar, yet we have left the truth unspoken. We know the power of prejudice to distort, yet we have let bigotry go unchallenged. We know the power of selfishness to seduce, yet we have let its grip go untested. True, we have not committed *all* the evils we deplore, but neither have we condemned them. We choose to be eye-winkers rather than whistle-blowers: to play it safe rather than straight; to promote harmony rather than justice; to heed the will of our neighbors rather than the word of our Lord.

We pray for mercy, O Lord, for having squandered our opportunities for bringing your rule to earth. And we pray not only for the release of our neighbors from the influence of our example, but for our own transformation: that, henceforth, when they do as we do, they will also be doing as we say; and that we and they might work together to turn your gifts into the foundation of that better world for which we pray.

❦ *Sunday Between August 7 and August 13.*

O God, you know all things and are not destroyed; you understand all things and are not desolate. For that which is destroyed you re-create, and that which is made desolate you restore.

How we envy you your strength, O God. And how we despair of our fragility! Often what we know condemns us, confuses us, conquers us. Often what we understand is so overwhelming that we run from it, so isolating that we abandon it, so incomplete that we surrender it. Intellect strives to govern the heart, and the heart rebels; the heart struggles to rule the intellect, and the intellect resists. Common sense contends with sentiment, they vie for control. Little do they realize that neither of them alone is sufficient.

O God, we are the Joabs of this day. Sometimes we are loyal to our emotions, but only until our hearts begin to break; then we become hard in order to guard them from harm, never minding the injury our hardness inflicts. Then, at other times, our reason reigns supreme, but often at the cost of being only half of who we are. Unable to link thought and feeling, practicality and personality, it is not long before we have murdered a wayward Absalom, against the command of love.

Make us *whole*, Lord, and we will be strong. Send to us, as to David, your messenger. Remind us through her that life is short, that death approaches, that there is no time for the outcast to remain outside us, for the exiled to remain beyond us, for the banished to remain against us. Your word will open the way between our head and our heart, that we might extend our hands without judgment *and* without folly. Your word will enable us to re-create what has been destroyed and to restore what has been made desolate. Yes, speak to us your word and, unlike Joab, we shall try to find a way to deal gently with Absalom—for your sake and for ours.

❧ <u>*Sunday Between August 14 and August 20.*</u>   O God, our feeble cry escapes our lips. Let it reach your ear!

We bear witness before you: Upon earth, this is the day of distress. We have walked abroad, and where once we strolled through paradise, we tiptoe now on the edge of the abyss. Earth's life passes away like smoke, its bones burn like a furnace. Its heart is withered like dry grass. It forgets to eat all but ashes, it forgets to drink all but tears.

The body of this earth bears witness to the reality of death. We run to you with the message, we want to be of help; but we tremble. Have we the courage to confess that all is not well in Eden?

A battle rages, and life has been lost. We stand before David the king, the parent, our friend—and he asks us, "Is it well with Absalom?" And though we have witnessed a terrible scene, though we have pleaded to carry the news, though we have run fast and hard to arrive with the word before a simple stranger—now, in his presence, our courage falters. We lack the strength to label sin, to name misfortune, to grieve death. And so we stand aside, and the sorry message falls without sympathy from another's lips.

O God, our cry is feeble, but no cry can be so feeble that you do not hear. Incline your ear! Listen to us, that we might find the strength to heed the warnings we have heard. Do not hide your face! Look upon us, that we might find the courage to face the abominations we have seen.

For yours, O Lord, is this earth; yours, its creatures, and all that dwells therein. You are its ruler, and you love it greatly. And so, Creator, answer us speedily, answer us mightily; and in all haste and with all power we shall do your bidding, that all might deal gently with Absalom!

🍁 *Sunday Between August 21 and August 27.* O Lord, you unveil hidden things. You make clear misunderstood things. You revive forgotten things. You, O Lord, are the Great Revealer—the mysterious bard, the strange troubadour of love, the storyteller spinning wondrous tales of a great devotion, the poet composing a universe where the Creator romances creation.

You are the revealer of the eternal Word, but you do not reveal the Word to the world, once and for all time. Again and again it is sung and told and spun and lived. And while with each unveiling we behold something old and familiar, with each disclosure we also witness something new and peculiar. You fashion the Word to its age and its place. If it is to be sung, you wrap its tune around a contemporary beat. If it is to be told, you narrate the plot in a native tongue. If it is to be embodied, you sculpt its face in a fitting image.

Something old, something new—your revelation, O God, is at once eternal and momentary, at once complete and fragmentary. On it goes and forever it comes, as it always has gone, as it always shall come again.

But we, like your first disciples, are unprepared for your revelation. We look for a savior: We want a new law, so long as it runs only so deep as the engravings on a stone tablet; we demand a new revelation, so long as it retains enough of the old that few changes are required. But this Jesus—his law cuts beneath tablets and appearances to lifeblood; his revelation is fulfilled not only in life, but in death.

Like the disciples, we have little depth of understanding. We hear, and we say, "This is a hard saying; who can listen to it?" We murmur and argue and grumble and debate, for we cannot agree with one another, and this revelation does not agree with us. We want something simple, and this is an enigma. We want wisdom, and this seems folly. We want blessing, and this is sacrifice.

O Lord, help us to persevere. We fear that many of us will draw back, that we will refuse to go farther from the old truths and the old ways than we have already gone. Endow us with the courage of Peter, that we might confess that we are lost without you, that we have no truth without abiding in you, that we have no way without following you.

O Lord, send your Spirit! Open us to your singing and your speaking and your sending it *this* day; lest, in not seeing it today, we be blind to it tomorrow.

❦ *Sunday Between August 28 and September 3.* O God, your word of centuries ago reaches our ears, speaking in accents that are all too clear, of issues that are all too familiar, and of people we know all too well.

"Be doers of the word, and not hearers only, deceiving yourselves," James cries. Writing to first-century Christians, he might have been invoking the heroic image of Simon Peter—not the fisherman, but the disciple; not the slavish traditionalist, but the emancipated reformer. At his best, Peter was more than a follower of Jesus: He was your servant. At his best, he was quick to hear and slow to speak, honoring you with his heart as with his lips. At his best, he was not merely a hearer of your word; he was a doer of your word. At his best, Peter did not deny you, as he had thrice denied Jesus; he was prepared to die for you. At his best, Peter did die for you. So, too, according to tradition, did James and John and, after them, a whole host of martyrs and reformers through the centuries.

We *know*, O Lord, that faithfulness is no guarantor of reward. We *know* that righteousness is no bestower of blessings. We *know* that truth is no guardian against calamity. We *know* that love is no protector from hatred. We *know* that good does not always repay good; evil does not always find penalty. Yet how often we have thought, "We must be faithful; we can work ourselves through the gates of heaven." Thus, we have sometimes done your word with motives less than pure. Who among us would dare number ourselves among the sheep?[20]

The author of James knew full well the dangers in store for those who are quick not only to hear your word but also to do it. Yet he boldly cried: "Do not be deceived! Be doers of the word, and not hearers only." Issued from the depths of a threatened church, yet dispatched

---

20. See Matthew 25:32-33.

from the heights of love, that cry took wing and flew through all of Christendom. O God, let it fly this day to us.

❧ *Sunday Between September 4 and September 10.*

O God, you endow us with gifts that go largely unused, you woo us with expectations that go largely unmet and you pursue us with offers that go largely unanswered. You astound us with your attention; apart from it, we would deem ourselves of little significance. Yet we dare not esteem lightly those whom you esteem highly, downgrade those whom you upgrade, or expect little of those from whom you demand much. So, instead of debating our value, we choose simply to thank you. We thank you for your gracious gifts, your lofty expectations, and your relentless offers—for loving us too deeply and too dearly to leave us alone.

If only we could say that, as you have loved us, so have we loved you. But we cannot. You instruct us with your testimonies, your statutes, your precepts, and your laws, but we ignore your teaching. Hearing, we hear not. You seek to enlighten us with your understanding, your insights, your words, and your wisdom, but we prefer the darkness to the light. Seeing, we see not. You challenge us with the commandments of your lawgivers and the oracles of your prophets, but we choose to be hearers rather than proclaimers of the word. Speaking, we speak not.

We live in a world that is often deaf, blind, and mute. For this we are deeply sorry, but we have helped to make it so. By our action and by our inaction, we have aggravated its afflictions. We have closed our ears to its harsh noises, shielded our eyes from its ugly sights, and remained tongue-tied before its vile deeds.

O Lord, take away not only our guilt but the indifference that allows us to remain as we are—and to like it. Create in us a clean heart and a right mind, so that, as the world's sounds grow loud, our hearing will grow sharp; so that, as the world's sights grow hideous, our seeing will grow perceptive; and so that, as the world's mischief-makers grow powerful, our speaking will grow bold. Unstop our ears, O God, that we might hear the cries for justice. Open our eyes, that we might recognize the scars of oppression. And loose our tongues, that justice might find its voice and oppressors get their due.

Recalling the futility of pious words unaccompanied by righteous deeds, we pray for the wisdom to speak truly and the strength to act decisively. Let our deeds speak so loudly that the hearers of *our* words will become the doers of your *word*.

❧ *Sunday Between September 11 and September 17.*

O God, whose name is above every name, we invoke your presence with mingled joy and hesitation: with joy, because we know that, before we turn in your direction, you have already turned in ours; yet with hesitation, because we also know that, as we have been quick to claim you as our heavenly parent, we have been slow to claim our neighbors as sisters and brothers. Despite our smallness, you have not withheld your name or your presence. Unwilling to accept the nay of yesterday as a nay for today, you pursue us with a grace and a patience beyond anything we deserve or understand. For this, O Lord, we adore you.

Face to face with your love, as undeniable as it is undeserved, we lament our failure to give it to others as freely as we receive it from you. Although we are unworthy of your love, we demand that others be worthy of ours. We define *worth* in terms not of your gospel but of our culture. We ignore the scriptural warning against showing partiality and bestow favor on those who earn what we earn, live as we live, vote as we vote, cater to the people to whom we cater, and shun the people whom we shun.

We act as if we would be content to be known by Jesus' name while mocking his values. As if his concern for the despised Samaritans held no significance, we continue to curse the enemies of our ancestors. As if his rebuke of the money-changers had no relevance, we continue to build our crystal cathedrals. As if his praise of peacemakers were of no consequence, we continue to worry more about the size of our arsenals than the supplies in our granaries. As if his warning against the bartering of our souls were of little moment, we continue to treat crossbearing as an option for those who cannot succeed in moneymaking.

For misunderstanding and misrepresenting you, O Lord, we ask your forgiveness. And we pray that here, as in Nazareth of Galilee, you will so open our eyes to the truth of Christ that we will understand him rightly and represent him faithfully.

❧ *Sunday Between September 18 and September 24.*

Gracious God, the source of life and everything that increases its value, we adore you for all you are and all you do, not only for us but also for all your children.

While grateful for all your gifts, we thank you, in particular, for the concerns that bind all humanity into a common family—the concerns through which you have turned the good earth into a global village and linked us together in a chain that, if broken, could spell ruin for us all. As we ponder these concerns, we are deeply troubled. At times, we second-guess you for saddling us so quickly with so great a responsibility. It is too heavy for us, demanding more strength than we possess and greater wisdom than we command. Yet we do thank you, O Lord. We thank you for having placed in us a trust to match our responsibility; for not abandoning us to *our* strength and *our* wisdom; and, for bestowing on our generation, as on no other, the rich legacy of human achievement.

We must confess, O Lord, that we have not done justice by this heritage. Not only have we disgraced some of its noblest values. We have left untouched vast stores of its traditions. Non-Christian religions have been dismissed with a wave of the hand. Economic systems different from our own have been treated with thinly veiled contempt. Customs preceding the industrial revolution have been described as uncivilized and their practitioners denounced as savages. This catalog of shame could be greatly extended, but we will not aggravate our guilt by dwelling on it. Not that we seek a verdict of innocence on our past. We pray, rather, for the strength and courage and wisdom not to repeat it.

Open our hearts to the influence of your spirit, O God, that we might open our minds to the influence of other traditions. Help us respect the culture of others—its history, its religion, its education, its economy, its politics, its institutions—as we would have them respect ours; to approach it not with sympathy but with empathy; and not to speak *of* it without speaking *for* it.

We pray, O God, for the enlightenment and empowerment of all peoples. We pray for the grace to remove the cloud of self-righteousness with which we have obscured other races and nations. Help us raise their self-esteem by the respect with which we deal with them; to heighten their regard for justice, by the passion with which we contend for their rights; and to intensify their hatred of oppression, by our support for the oppressed. Let us so represent you to one another that you might reveal yourself in us all.

❧ *Sunday Between September 25 and October 1.* Eternal God, in every age you have entered into covenant, and in no age have you been without a covenant people. We praise your holy name, not because you have broken covenant with others to make covenant with us, but because you have made your covenant to include us.

We are grateful, dear Lord, for fellow members of the covenant—for all our co-workers in your service. Without them, not only would your mission go unaccomplished, but we could never enjoy the abundant life you promised. We need one another. For without our mutual exchange—the continuing dialogue that enables us to learn from one another's mistakes and to profit from one another's experience—we would pose an even greater obstacle to your cause than we do. We pray, therefore, that you will deepen our awareness of and our appreciation for one another.

When we think of the ways we have impeded the work of our co-laborers, we have enough guilt to go around. There is much we should have done that we failed to do. And there is much we did that we should not have done. We should have accepted those by whose side we labored, but they could not be true disciples of Christ, we seemed to feel, unless they thought as we thought, felt as we felt, and acted as we acted.

O Lord, as we look to the future, we ask you to clean the slate. Let us recall your teaching in Nazareth of Galilee: that it is more blessed to give than to receive; that we must lose our lives to save them; and that how we love is more important than what we believe. While you are no longer here to enflesh these words, your Spirit is not absent. Let it cease to be merely a presence of which we may take notice if we choose; make it a force with which we must come to terms.

O Christ, teach us to surround our jealousy for your name with respect and with reverence. Deliver us from the impulse to give ultimate answers to questions concerning immediate needs: When the sick come to us in need of medicine, the homeless in need of housing, the hungry in need of food, or the jobless in need of work, grant us the wisdom to recognize that true evangelism puts humanity before religion, and the grace to acknowledge that true religion takes people more seriously than it takes itself.

Above all, O Lord, we pray for purity of heart—for the will to will one thing alone; for the will so to love that we will give ourselves for the world—the world for which you died.

🍁 *Sunday Between October 2 and October 8.*   O God, how you test us! Even as the Pharisees and the disciples tested Jesus, you test us! You put to us the same choice that they put to him: Shall we cling to our pride and seek to achieve our salvation? Or shall we trust your grace and dare to receive our salvation? Shall we accept your gift, or shall we reject it, thinking we must earn our due?

As if any human being could boast in your presence—the one by whose word the universe is designed! As if any laws that we might decree could be righteous in your presence—the one from whose mind true law is derived! As if any obedience to such laws could be perfect in your presence—the one by whose character perfection is defined!

We know, O God, that it is not obedience to rules that brings us to paradise. It is our ability to be grasped by your grace. Learn about grace, you have said, from the children. Learn from them about salvation. Their happiness depends not on strict rules but stable relationships. They learn more from forgiveness than from obedience. They receive as easily as they give—they can receive without earning and give without owing.

Better than we, children understand the oneness of the world, the give-and-receive of the world, the gifts and the givers of the world. By contrast, we have grown up: Common sense prevails, old habits win out. We live by the law that you cannot get without giving. Somehow we must find the child within, and, holding its hand, we must save ourselves and our world. We must save ourselves and our world not only by moving within the freedom of your grace, but also by abandoning the pride that will not let us budge.

Let us see our children, Lord! Let us see our children's children!

❧ *Sunday Between October 9 and October 15.* O God, how hard it is to enter your kingdom! Its gates open among us, but they are not easy to spy. Its heralds sit among us, but they are not easy to spot. We rely on what we see and overlook the mysteries of the unseen. We depend on what we hear and neglect the secrets of the silent.

Your revelation offers us clues in our search, Lord, but they often seem contradictory. In one breath you whisper, "Become like children!" In the next you confide, "You must move beyond your youth!"

You told our parents, "You shall love the Lord your God with all your heart, and with all your soul, and with all your might. And these words which I command you this day shall be upon your heart; and you shall teach them diligently to your children."[21] And yet you have told us, "Leave your parents and your homes, and follow me."

We have much to learn, O God. In childhood, in innocence, without deep understanding of good and evil, standing only on the foundation of right and wrong that our parents have laid: Here we learn about obedience and self-discipline. But you would have us grow in spirit as we grow in body. Therefore, in age, in maturity, our understandings of the good and evil that lay without *and* within us must deepen. And, as they deepen, they will seek a foundation firmer than the rules of childhood. For what child can believe that good behavior will not be rewarded, that bad behavior will not be punished? Yet *we* know that the rain falls upon the good and the evil alike. And what child can count the cost of discipleship? Yet many of *us* have walked away from you in dismay, unable to surrender into your hands what we esteem most highly.

In childhood we learn much about obedience, O God. But those of us who learn its lessons best will one day have all the more to learn about forgiveness and grace. The greater our confidence in our obedience, the greater our danger of pride. The greater our awareness of our own righteousness, the dimmer our awareness of sin. The greater our allegiance to our own laws, O God, the weaker our adherence to your will.

Help us grow up, Lord. We would leave everything and follow you, but we are feeble. The best of what we have, the greatest of what we believe ourselves to be—we have reckoned it as your blessing upon our faithfulness. But we are no longer children. Look upon us with love and remind us, "No one is good but God alone." Look upon us with love, and challenge us, "If your spirit is strong, give *all* that you have, and follow me."

Look upon us with mercy, O Lord, not with judgment; and inspire in us the strength to step beyond the world of law to the world of love, where faithful existence is not for our own gain but for your glory.

❧ *Sunday Between October 16 and October 22.*   O God, who shows us how to serve through the service of Jesus Christ, look upon us with understanding. We have dedicated ourselves to the service of folly; and finally, in the noontide of our foolishness, we have the gall to ask with the sons of Zebedee, "Teacher, we want you to do for us *whatever we ask of you.*"

---

21. See Deuteronomy 6:5-7.

In the high noon of your infinite mercy, you ask, "What do you want me to do for you?" Unrepentant, we muster the further audacity not to ask, but to *demand*, "Grant us to sit beside you in your glory." When you gently warn that we do not know what we are asking, we are impudent enough to claim, "We are able to drink the cup that you drink, and to be baptized with the baptism with which you are baptized." You are right, Lord; we do not know what we ask, for the cup is filled with the wine of servanthood, and the baptism is unto sacrifice—even to the point of suffering. And that service, that sacrifice, *is* your glory.

We do not understand, but you do. And so, you are patient. You tolerate our prideful indiscretions, our arrogant presumptions. And then, you take up your teaching again, for it is plain that we do not yet understand what greatness resides in the choice to be servant, what majesty abides in the choice to be least.

Forgive our slow learning, God. Forgive our blustery confidence that erupts in speech when silence would be better, yet holds its tongue when one word could be decisive. And forgive our haughty swaggering, that struts amidst the weak when kneeling would be better, yet bends the knee when one step could be forever.

We ask your forgiveness, O Lord, in the name of the One who came not to be served but to serve. We ask forgiveness, that by your great mercy we might find that we *are* able, despite and because of who we are.

❀ *Sunday Between October 23 and October 29.*

O Christ, you are our great interceder! Even as mighty forces in our world conspire to tear us apart, your powerful spirit schemes to reconcile us. You are the herald of this, your homecoming—the bringing in of the blind, the opening up of the closed-minded, the softening up of the hardhearted, the lifting up of the downtrodden. And the reunion continues to this day—in this life and the next.

We confess our need for reunion, Lord. And we concede that we stand with a foot on either side of the fence. On the one side, we number ourselves among the blind and the downtrodden, among the exiled and the excluded. In different ways each of us has known the pain of being shut out. The isolation, the frustration, the exasperation of being told and shown that we do not belong, that we are not wanted—it has frozen into a hard core in the center of our existence, and soon we have become too afraid to care anymore, to share anymore.

On the other side, we number ourselves among the closed-minded and the hardhearted, among those who banish and bar. In different ways each of us has shut someone out. By word and deed we have isolated, frustrated, and exasperated our neighbors, letting them know that they do not belong, that they are not wanted. Our cruelty has hardened into a cold stone in the center of our existence, and soon we have become too blind to care anymore, to share anymore.

Yes, we confess our need for reunion, Lord. But before we can reunite with others, we must reunite our different selves. That within us which we guard must be relinquished; that which we deny must be owned. We must come home from our inner exile before we can return from the outer.

Heal our sight that we might behold ourselves clearly. If we have long been blinded by fantasies of our own greatness, as were James and John, open our eyes to our arrogance. If we have long been blinded by fears of our own flaws, as was Bartimaeus, reveal to us our timidity. Do not rebuke us for asking for vision, as your disciples rebuked the pleading beggar, but grant us the greatness that comes with humility and the courage that overcomes weakness.

Heal our sight, O Lord, and we shall declare: We have heard of you by the hearing of the ears, but now our eyes see you. And we shall praise your name, saying: You have heard our cry and delivered us from all our fears!

❦ _Sunday Between October 30 and November 5._   Creator God, incline your ear to our hearts, for they long for you. Send your song to our souls, for they wait for you. Whisper your mysteries to our minds, for they search for you. Match your purposes to our strengths, for they rest in you. O God who hears and serenades us, who inspires and moves us, hear our prayer!

Creator God, you fashion us from the earth. Made of the dust, we are tossed about by the wind; we are scattered around and trampled underfoot. Then, when all is done, we return to the dust from which we come. Such is the clay of which we are made.

And yet, you breathe _your_ breath into our nostrils. Quickened by your spirit, we command the winds; we rise above the storm and utter, "Be still!" And, when all is done, we return to the spirit from which we come. Such is the soul of which we are formed.

What cryptic creatures we are, such a mix of this world and the next!

And yet *we* are the ones who presume to ask the questions of *you;* we are the ones who dare to doubt. We are the skeptics and the cynics trying to trap you in our snares of reason and rebellion.

Are we really different from the chief priests and the elders, whose anxiety about human authority exceeded their respect for your authority?[22] Are we really different from the Pharisees and the Herodians, whose worry about Caesar transcended their worship of you? Are we really different from the Sadducees, whose concern about the future life dwarfed their interest in the present life?

No, Lord, we are not so different. The chief priest rules, the elder advises, the Pharisees and Herodians and Sadducees argue within us from morning till night. We walk out of the door at dawn, and we must decide until dusk, "What is right? What is correct? What is best? What is *just?*"

O God, give us more than wisdom. Grant us the understanding of the scribe, who put a question to Jesus not in suspicion but in faith. Let us ask, with him, "Which commandment *is* the first of all?" And when you answer, "Love me, and love *them,*" opening your arms wide to the world, let us find the courage to say, "You are right, Teacher!" And even though you have given us more than we requested—not one commandment but two, not twice as hard but ninety-times-nine—let us exclaim, "Yes! You *are* right!" Even though you express not ceremonial but *personal* concerns, let us vow, "Yes—to love you and to love one's neighbor as oneself, it *is* much more than all offerings and sacrifices!"

To gain this understanding, to walk in this path—this is the purpose for which you have made us. From the dust of the earth and the breath of heaven, you have fashioned us not in the image of the chief priests or the elders, but in *your* image—and in the image of this scribe, who was not far from your kingdom.

❦ *Sunday Between November 6 and November 12.*

O God, hear our prayer! For the story of the widow commended by Jesus has convicted us! It has shined upon the shadowy reaches of our souls, bringing to light our hunger for glory and our passion for power; our secret longing to stand out in and above the crowd; our terrible

---

22. References in this paragraph are to the three tests put to Jesus by these groups just prior to the scribe's question in Mark 12:28.

need to prove ourselves worthy before the world by appearing to be worthy before you.

We gather weekly to worship you, to give you praise and offerings, but this day you greet us with a shattering word:

"Who requires of you this trampling in my courts?" you thunder. "Bring no more vain offerings. I cannot endure iniquity and solemn assembly. Your feasts, my soul hates; they have become a burden to me, I am weary of bearing them. When you spread forth your hands, I will hide my eyes from you; even though you make many prayers, I will not listen.

"Wash yourselves! Make yourselves clean; cease to do evil, learn to do good; seek justice, correct oppression; *defend the orphan, plead for the widow,*" you cry.[23]

This is what you require, Lord. Your voice drowns our every sermon and prayer and song with the reminder, "Let there be no joy without justice, no rejoicing without righteousness!"

Woe to us, O God, for we have not done what we have preached, we have not meant what we have prayed![24] We have cleaned the outside of the cup without first cleaning the inside; we are like whitewashed tombs filled with dead bones.

Woe to us, for we have laid heavy burdens on other shoulders while refusing to touch them with our own hands!

Woe to us, for we have sought places of honor while leaving others in places of harm!

Woe to us, for we have built shrines for yesterday's prophets and monuments for yesterday's saints, while crucifying the prophets and stoning the saints of today!

Woe to us, for we have traversed land and sea to make a single convert, only to make that convert twice as much a child of misery as ourselves!

Woe to us, for we have stood outside the gates of your kingdom to bar another from entering!

Woe to us, for we have tithed sweetly, offering up herbs and spices, while neglecting the weightier matters of justice and mercy and faith!

O God of the forsaken, we deem ourselves virtuous, but the example of the widow has declared us villains. While we have stood off at a dis-

---

23. See Isaiah 1:12-17.
24. The following lines are based on Matthew 23.

tance, Jesus has commended the widow of Jerusalem for taking a leap of faith; for offering up all she possesses at the risk of her life, putting to shame those who tithe out of their abundance. While we have stood off at a distance, Jesus has watched her give away her last coin; at the risk of her own welfare, she has surrendered all she has for the welfare of others.

O God, what sacrifices she has made with her life while we have tithed in the temple! Those two copper coins—so insignificant in themselves, gifts smaller than the smallest, yet greater than the greatest!

We have sinned, Lord, and we scatter from you, having seen the truth of what we do and who we are. Gather us gently together again, as a hen gathers her brood under her wings, and we shall come in! For this day we shout with one voice, "Blessed are the prophets! Blessed are the widows! Blessed are they who come in the name of the Lord!"

❦ *Sunday Between November 13 and November 19.*

O God, we give thanks to you! We proclaim the glory of your kingdom! We tell of your power! We declare to all the world your mighty deeds and glorious splendor!

We bless your name, Lord, for by your grace are we saved; by your mercy, forgiven; by your forbearance, accepted; by your love, restored! And by this grace are we made gracious; and by this mercy, merciful; and by this forbearance, forbearing; and by this love, loving!

This is so—not because of anything we have done, but because of what *you* have done! As the author of Hebrews declared, "Every priest stands daily at services, offering repeatedly the same sacrifices, which can never take away sins." But Jesus Christ, once and for all, embodied our relationship with you. And the Holy Spirit works at all times to write its Good News upon our hearts. Yes, our salvation is already accomplished, not by our acts, but by your act—not in another world, but in this world; not in another time, but in this time. All this you have promised.

And still more. For in your boundless love, you have vowed, "I will remember your sins and misdeeds no more." All is done, all is forgiven—even before our wavering, even before our failing, even before our pleading, even before our trembling. How can we not bless your name!

Yours is a name terrible in its mystery. We do not know what visage lies behind it. Hannah saw you as the One who set the world on the pillars of the earth, and as the One who brings low the mighty and lifts high the meek. Isaiah conceived you as "Mother"; he uttered your word to Israel, "Can a woman forget her sucking child, that she should have no compassion on the child of her womb? I will not forget you!"[25] And Jesus regarded you as "Father"; he told of your provision even for the birds of the air and the lilies of the field.[26]

Who are you, O God, who remembers your creatures, but no more their sin? You are everything and no-thing. You are the terrifying door into the unknown and the comforting embrace at the threshold!

O Lord, we call upon your name, which is above every name and gives meaning to all names. Usher us through that door, and we shall serve you, whose realm is eternal and whose dominion is everlasting!

❋ *Last Sunday After Pentecost.*   Eternal God, who was and is and is yet to be, we bow before you in awe and adoration. When life pushes us into a corner, we run from you only to find that from you there is no escape—that, no matter how we get off the course, you will not let us off the hook. For this, dear Lord, we are grateful. How good it is to know that we are loved by anybody. Yet how much better it is to know that the One who loves us, above all others, is the God of creation and the Lord of history—the Savior of the world and the ruler of the universe.

For centuries we have hailed you as our God and called ourselves your people. We have worshiped you as King of kings and called all other monarchs your agents. Yet we have not judged their rule by yours, measured their law by yours, or tested their teaching by yours. Confronted by your demand for a clear-cut either/or, we have opted for Caesar's offer of a both/and. Face to face with Caesar's agents, we have taken the path of least resistance. When they weighted the scales of justice on the side of the strong, we were not blind, yet we remained silent. When they raised the costs of education beyond the reach of the masses, we recognized the inequity, yet we remained silent. When they inflated the price of political office in favor of the rich, we saw the danger, yet we remained silent. If only we could plead ignorance!

But we were not ignorant—only silent. We had already begun to see the handwriting on the wall. We knew even then that the cost of our

25. Inspired by Isaiah 49:15.
26. See Matthew 6:25-26.

compromise would run high and one day compromise your rule. Now that the day for payment is at hand, we will not insult you by pleading either ignorance or innocence, for we are as guilty as sin. We were aware, O Lord, that your dominion is not of this world. Yet we have behaved as if it were. We betrayed you, but you were not the only victim. There were others, many others: not only those who looked to us for guidance, but also those whom we might have led to look to you.

Grant us, O Lord, the courage to put our sin behind us even as you have put it behind you. Help us, henceforth, so to live as to bear witness to the truth for which Christ lived and died and still lives. Guide us by your spirit that our neighbors, when they turn to us, will find clarity in the midst of confusion; support, in the midst of sorrow; unity, in the midst of division; purpose, in the midst of aimlessness; and you, in the midst of despair. So fill us with your love that we might become temporal witnesses to your eternal rule. Let us hope that, as a consequence, the rulers of this world will accept your rule—a rule that is not of this world.

Year C

O Anointer of Prophets,

Long have the seas roared, and long have we cried out, but the sound of our cries has been drowned by crashing waves and screaming winds. Only the battered earth has cupped an ear to hearken to our lament. Long have the mountains quaked, and long have we moaned, but our moans have been buried beneath cracking rocks and splitting timbers. Only the trembling earth has reached out to grasp our hand.

The earth has been a witness to our suffering, Lord, and she has also been its victim. If our hearts have been weighted down with the cares of this life, hers has been crushed by the cares of our lives.

But now the burden has become too great. Our battles have bent her shoulders. Our quarrels have broken her back. Her face is disfigured, her body scarred. She stumbles, and falls; she can carry us no farther. We kneel over her: Her pulse is weak, the rivers are running dry; her breathing is shallow, the breezes are blowing ill.

We call upon you, Lord! Still the waves and calm the winds! Silence the rocks and hush the timbers! This earth cannot save us; like her inhabitants, she must be saved.

Help her, O Lord, by helping us! Raise up a healer among us to restore the earth! Call a prophet to announce your reign! Send a savior to reveal your love! Choose a servant to render your justice! Anoint a messiah to redeem your world!

We are watching, Lord! In all times, in all places, we watch for a sign that your Coming One is drawing near. We keep the vigil for ourselves and for the earth, for we must know the time of our visitation.

A new earth is leaping in the womb, Lord; a new humanity is kicking beneath your hand. Won't you deliver your messiah? We wait. We wonder. We watch.

❧ *First Sunday of Advent*

Advent Season

❧ *Second Sunday of Advent.* O God, you hold creation close to your heart. As you have loved her into being, your heart has been deeply wounded by her pain and wonderfully mended by her joy. From beginning to end, from small to great, from low to high, from near to far, from first to last, you have cared for her, tending her needs, sustaining her growth, easing her suffering, increasing her pleasure.

Then, having been fashioned by your hands and inspired by your breath, creation has surrounded us—to tend *our* needs, sustain *our* growth, ease *our* suffering, and increase *our* pleasure. This you have intended from the beginning, for you hold us, like her, close to your heart. You have entrusted us to her care because you have looked upon her and declared her good; and, at the same time, you have entrusted her to *our* care, for while capable of doing good, we must learn how through time and toil.

So you mean us to be partners in the gospel, Lord—partners with you, with creation, with one another. You mean us to partake together of the grace, the mercy, the abundance of this world. But the partnership has been broken—not because you have failed to hold us up, not because creation has let us down, but because we have proved unequal to—or worse, unmindful of—the task.

It was all you have ever asked of us, Lord—right offerings and good fruits. But we have kept the best offerings and ripest fruits for ourselves, while you have waited and creation has wasted away. We have frantically hoarded while our world has been depleted. We have leisurely washed our hands while our world has been defiled. We have hastened to endless feasts while our world has been denied. We have reveled without a care while our world has been raped. We have not noticed nature's need, but ignored it; not sustained her growth, but stunted it; not eased her suffering, but sharpened it; not increased her pleasure, but diminished it.

O God, save us all from one another, and save your world from our sin! Hear our cry! Send a savior who is one of us, who can understand us, and show us the way! We hearken to your word, Lord; we await the sounds of your coming! Do not forget us; do not delay!

❧ *Third Sunday of Advent.* O Lord our God, where a rainbow bends in the midst of thunder, or a flower blooms in the midst of sand, you are there. Where a dream persists in the midst of conflict, or a protest arises in the midst of calm, you are there. Where a candle glows in the midst of winter, or a river thaws in the midst of spring, you are there. Where a cradle rocks in the midst of suffering, or a hand is held in the midst of pain, you are there. Where a prayer ascends in the midst of cursing, or passion flares in the midst of uncaring, you are there.

O God, you are in our midst. And because you are here, you tell us, "Do not fear; let not your hands grow weak." But we are not so easily comforted; we are not so quickly inspired. You surround us, but we cannot see your face, we cannot hear your voice, we cannot feel your embrace. How can we trust you? How can we have courage? How can our hands be strong?

We confess this, Lord: We would rather trust ourselves. We would rather venerate our past—our pride in family lines, honored traditions, historic institutions. We would rather glorify our future—our opportunity for posterity, prosperity, and popularity. When we implore, "What shall we do?" we do not ask one of your locust-eating, leather-girdled prophets, who would summon us to the wilderness and demand that we change our ways![1] Instead, we ask the keepers of our law, the caretakers of our culture, and the custodians of our religion, for we know that their answers will be pleasing to the taste. Their answers shall become *our* answers, dripping like honey from our tongues but falling like vinegar on your ears.

O Lord, how merciful you are for not forsaking us! You send us messenger after messenger, only to be mocked, and word after word, only to be despised.[2] Now your greatest messenger is about to be born, a messenger who not only will speak and do your word, but embody it. Do you know what you do? We can smile at a baby, but shall we not scorn the man? We can shelter the child, like a hen gathering her chicks under her wings, but shall we shelter the Christ, or hide in the upper room?[3]

O God, you send this child into our midst to make your presence among us tangible, visible, touchable. But will the child make you understandable, *acceptable* to the stoners and killers of prophets, to us who so easily become afraid, whose weak hands so quickly seek to cru-

---

1. See Matthew 3:4.
2. See II Chronicles 36:15-16.
3. Inspired by Matthew 23:37.

cify? Can truth really walk safely among the deceitful; or justice, among the vengeful; or love, among the hateful; or grace, among the spiteful?

Help us to trust you, Lord. We cannot comprehend this thing that is about to happen, this baby who will be our savior. We have learned well how we can be custodians of law, guardians of culture, and champions of religion; we do not know how—or if—we can be disciples of such a one as this. Prepare us for the bearer of the gospel, O God, lest we receive the Good News as *bad* news, and turn our backs.

Be with us, Lord, as you send him to us. The thunder rumbles: Lead us to the bending rainbow. The sands creep: Lead us to the blooming flower. The winter blows: Lead us to the glowing candle. The spring breaks: Lead us to the thawing river.

The suffering one comes: Lead us to the rocking cradle!

❦ *Fourth Sunday of Advent.* O God, your light is rising in the east. Some say it is a star, announcing the birth of a new ruler. Others believe it is the sun, breaking the dawn of a new age. Whatever it may be, this glorious event is of your doing, for from the beginning your hand has hung the great lights in the heavens.

The light has not yet arrived; its time is not yet come, but we await its coming with fear and with joy.

Fear—that the pride you have promised *then* to scatter is but the arrogance within us. Fear—that the might you have promised *then* to humble is but the cruelty within us. Fear—that the wealth you have promised *then* to spurn is but the greediness within us. Fear—that this light shall reveal what we have concealed, and challenge what we need to change.

Yet our trembling is mixed with rejoicing. Joy—that scarred hearts might love again. Joy—that downcast eyes might look up again. Joy—that empty mouths might eat again. Joy—that idle hands might work again. Joy—that tired spirits might play again.

We are afraid, and we are joyful, because when this light finally breaks in the east, signaling a new ruler, or a new age, or both, this world will be seen in a new way. What *is* will begin to disappear into the realm of what *was*. What was hoped for will begin to appear in the sphere of what can be. Old ones will hear and be born again. Little ones will speak with the wisdom of sages. First will be last, and last, first. High will be low, and low, high. Every fettered slave will be released, and all will serve your cause in freedom. Every blinded eye will receive sight, and all will gaze upon your face with love.

O Lord, soon your light will hover above the place where Mary lies. As we approach her, remove the density of our fear and increase the intensity of our joy. Lay our hand upon her, ever so gently, that we might greet the tiny messenger, the child come to do your will when we would not, or could not. Run our hand across her sweating brow, ever so slowly, for you would have us be the salt of earth. Lift our hand to feel her throat, filled with groans at the pangs of birth, even as we have groaned in travail until now, awaiting our salvation.[4]

Place our hand in Mary's, Lord. Let us touch her, that we might ease her suffering, and let her spirit touch us, that we might confess, with the shepherds and the magi who will join us at her side, "The child comes, and so have we."

4. Inspired by Mark 9:50; Romans 8:22-23.

Christmas Season

🍁 *Christmas Eve/Day.*   O God, we have waited long in the fields of night, keeping watch over the flocks, looking for signs of the morning. And what a sign you have given! The birth of a child! The birth of a savior! The birth of new life! Through your tender mercy, a new day has dawned, giving light to us who sit in darkness and dwell in the shadow of death, revealing the path of righteousness and guiding our feet into the way of peace.[5]

This child who has been born among us—he is the one with whom you will be well pleased.[6] And he has been born not among the mighty, but the lowly; not among the ruling, but the ruled; not among the rich, but the poor; not among the favored, but the outcast.

He is not the messiah we had expected from you, Lord. But there is the star dancing above the stall, and there is the angelic choir singing overhead: "Glory to God in the highest, and on earth, peace!" All creation celebrates the sign that has come to the nations, the salvation that has come to the peoples. The night has been broken; how can we doubt? The dawn is here; how can we not view the world in a different light?

We have run from the fields to see this thing that has happened; we have seen with our eyes—help us to understand with our hearts! O God, help us to know the time of our visitation, so that when the child, become a man, draws near to the place of our habitation, his heart might not be broken; that, instead of weeping, he might rejoice, saying, "Now you have learned the things that make for peace!"[7]

🍁 *First Sunday After Christmas.*   Great are the works of your hands, O God! They clothe you with honor and majesty, for they are faithful and just, promoting peace and sustaining life: You make the springs to give drink to the beasts and water the trees where birds build their nests. You cause the grass to grow for pasture and sow the seed for cultivation. You fill the sea with living things and speckle the sky with eagles.

Your works cover you with a garment of light, O God, for they are righteous and good, enduring forever: You set the earth on its foun-

5. See Luke 1:78-79.
6. See Luke 3:22.
7. Inspired by Luke 19:41-42.

dations, never to be shaken. You speak, and the mountains rise over the plain; you point, and the valleys sink to their appointed places. You order the moon to mark the seasons, and its countenance changes each passing night; you command the sun to part the days, and its face vanishes over the western horizon. You send forth your spirit, and we are created; you cry for joy, and the world is renewed.

Your works robe you in the raiment of power, O God, for they are worthy of remembrance, inspiring worship: Our praises rumble like raging waters through the mighty canyons, and soar like rushing wings toward the towering clouds, and sigh like gentle breezes through the ancient trees, and pound like galloping hooves across the windswept plains. In wisdom you have made the earth; in wisdom we shall fill the earth with rousing songs of gladness.

We will sing to you as long as we live; we will chant your praises while we have being. Like the boy Samuel, we will serve you; like the boy Jesus, we will seek you. Like both of them, we will ask the question that has been raised by your children throughout the ages, "What must we do, to be doing the works of God?" And you will answer as you have answered throughout the ages, "You shall give to others freely; you shall open wide your hands, and your hearts shall not be grudging, that I might bless you in all that you do."[8]

O one who prepared a stable for him who would have no place to lay his head, shelter us, that we might shelter others. O one who delivered him whom we would call the Great Physician, heal us, that we might heal others. O one who provided swaddling clothes for him whose robe would be gambled away, clothe us, that we might clothe others. O one who raised up teachers for him whom we would claim as our Great Teacher, guide us, that we might guide others.

Great are your works, O God, and great shall be our works if you are our Lord! Bless us, make us a faithful and just people, promoting peace and sustaining life, that the works of our hands might clothe you with honor and majesty! Make us a righteous and good people, enduring forever, that the works of our hearts might cover you with a garment of light! Make us a people worthy of remembrance, inspiring love, that the works of our spirits might robe you in the raiment of power![9]

---

8. See John 6:28; Deuteronomy 15:10-11.
9. Much imagery in this prayer has been taken from Psalm 104.

❧ *Second Sunday After Christmas.*   O Lord, in the beginning the Word came forth from your mouth and covered the earth like a morning mist. The earth, thirsting for life, opened her lips, and as she drank, living things sprang forth—deer on the land and dolphins in the sea, birds in the sky and beasts in the field. The mist watered the whole face of the ground, until the dust no longer blew in the wind; then you formed us from the clay, and breathed into our nostrils your holy breath.[10]

This is your story, O God—the glory of your creative Word, the Living Water, the Eternal Fount. Our mouths shout your name unto the heavens; our feet dance your dance upon the earth!

O Lord, in the beginning the Word came forth from your mouth and lit up the night like the noontime sun. The earth, groping in the darkness, squinted her eyes, and as she looked, mysterious things were revealed—the beauty of her face and the bounty of her life, the brevity of eternity and the boundary of infinity. The light shone through the gloom and eclipsed every shadow, and the night waged war, but could not overcome the light.

This is your story, O God—the glory of your revealing Word, the Light of the World, the Eternal Flame. Our mouths shout your name unto the heavens; our feet dance your dance upon the earth!

O Lord, the Word was with you in the beginning of the world. And now the world has begun anew, for you have caused the Word to come forth again. Now the world has been reborn, for the Word has come forth from the womb of Mary. The news has wrapped the earth in an angelic hymn; it has lighted the night with a royal star.

The Word has become flesh to dwell among us, full of grace and truth. Let the Word grow, O God, and let us receive him as Living Water, that our thirst might be satisfied. Let the Word grow, and let us receive him as the Light of the World, that our hearts might be illumined. Let the Word grow, and let us receive him as the Good Shepherd, that our feet might be led where none shall stumble.

This is your story, O God—the glory of your saving Word, the Keeper of the Fold, the Eternal Friend. Our mouths shout your name unto the heavens; our feet dance your dance upon the earth!

---

10. Inspired by Genesis 2:6-7.

Season After Epiphany

✤ *First Sunday After Epiphany (Baptism of the Lord).*
Almighty and eternal God, Lord of Christ, we bow before you in honor
of him who for our sake became one of us that we might become one
with you. Before his coming, O God, we most often listened for your
voice in the startling sounds of nature in upheaval—the crack of lightning, the blast of thunder, the roar of the tornado, the explosion of the
volcano, the whip of the hurricane.

But now, thanks to him, we have no excuse for being surprised when
your voice comes to us in hushed tones—claiming us as your children,
directing us to your task, humbling us in our strength, and consoling us
in our weakness. Thanks to him, we have no excuse for ignoring your
affirmation of us at our baptism, or for reducing the meaning of baptism to the words of a prescribed ritual. Let us not forget, O Lord, that
our public acknowledgment of kinship with you must ever be matched
by the private; that the outward sign must ever be matched by the
inward change it signifies; that the holy sacrament must ever be
matched by holy living.

We know, O Lord, that you do not address us as your beloved children lightly or unadvisedly. You did not greet Jesus as your child
because others pinned on him the lofty title of Messiah, but because he
embraced the lowly task of your servant. And you will not so greet us
until we claim his mission as enthusiastically as we claim his name,
until the decision to take the name of Jesus with us is joined by the
determination to take the love of Jesus with us. For the sake of your
people and ours, and for the sake of your joy and ours, we ask, O Lord,
for the courage to honor faithfully the Christ whose name we so often
take in vain.

When we survey the world around us, we behold a sea of faces troubled by a world in fateful transition, faces anxious for some assurance
that there is meaning in the struggle. Grant us the grace, O God, so to
proclaim your message of meaning that the troubled world will be comforted, the anxious consoled. Let us proclaim your message not by
echoing a heavenly voice but by performing earthly deeds; not by gaz-
ing at openings in the sky but by seizing opportunities on the ground;
not simply by calling for reliance on the Holy Spirit but by acting in
reliance on the Holy Spirit; not simply by inviting divine intervention
but by implementing human intention.

As we have been baptized in the name of Jesus Christ, baptize us now, O Lord, in the *cause* of Jesus Christ, until his mission becomes our mission and we perform it in his spirit.

✤ *Second Sunday After Epiphany.* O Lord, Vindicator of the abused, Redeemer of the oppressed, Refuge of the exiled, and Fortress of the besieged, we call you by all these names because we have experienced you in all these ways. When we were abused, you vindicated us; when we were oppressed, you redeemed us; when we were exiled, you sheltered us; and when we were besieged, you strengthened us. So we address you now, O God, as in times past our ancestors addressed you.

Your detractors would have us believe that we give you more credit than you are due. Determined to topple you from the throne of life, they call the roll of human beings who have justified us, set us free, made us safe, and kept us strong. Too captivated by human achievement to consider its source, they do not see you, unless you blind them with the rays of the noonday sun; they do not hear you, unless you deafen them with the roar of a waterfall; they do not feel you, unless you sweep them aside with the winds of a blizzard. But we know better, Lord: We do not look for you only in the sights that dazzle; we do not listen for you only in the sounds that deafen; we do not feel you only in the forces that overwhelm. We remember in whose image we are created, and we believe the presence that cannot be seen; we listen to the voice that cannot be heard; we grasp the hand that cannot be touched. We thank you, dear Lord, for delivering us from the skepticism that denies you because it cannot prove you, and from the dogmatism that affirms you because it *can* prove you.

When we consider the gifts with which you blessed the world through Jesus—concern for the weak and afflicted, compassion for the sick and imprisoned, love for the lowly and despised—we are amazed by how many of them are within our reach. You have made us but a little lower than yourself; you have set eternity within the heart of each of us and made the incarnation of your spirit a possibility for all of us. Yet your clear light, the light that shone so brilliantly yet so modestly in Jesus, condemns us even as it instructs us. Unlike Jesus, we seek not so much to serve as to impress our neighbors. As much as we might like to help others discover their gifts, we prefer to win praise by displaying our own. So the gifts that were meant to tie us together work to tear us apart, and our unity in diversity becomes bitterness in division.

O God, we turn to you in confession and supplication. Before you and our neighbors, we acknowledge our abuse of your gifts. Forgive us for exercising them without respect for your purpose in bestowing them. Help us to recognize that you call us to use our gifts—not that others might conceal theirs, but that others might reveal theirs; not that the abilities of some might be applauded, but that the abilities of all might be appreciated; not that the worth of individuals might be downgraded, but that the welfare of the community might be upgraded.

Dear Lord, we are especially mindful of those in the human community whose struggle for existence is so dominated by concern for clothing and shelter and bread that it has yet to become a struggle for meaning. Let us never forget that they are no less your children than we and that, just as you have blessed us with diverse gifts, so you have blessed them. So we pray that you will enable us to help them discover their gifts, that they might use them in your spirit for the common good.

❦ *Third Sunday After Epiphany.*   O God, whose majesty fills the heavens with glory and whose love floods the earth with meaning, we approach you in awe and gratitude, giving thanks that we are made in your image, called according to your purpose, and commissioned to do your will.

At times, we are overwhelmed by the difficulty of this commission. The distance between you and us is so great! But you never leave us without help. You bless us with guides and with guidance, sending into our midst lawgivers, prophets, priests, psalmists, sages, apostles, and missionaries. And you make *us* your witnesses, that we might revive the soul of the church, even as your law once revived the soul of Israel. We pray that, just as your guidance enabled Israel to fulfill her commission, it might now enable us to fulfill ours.

Forgive us, O Lord, for the selfish way we often accept your help. We are quick to claim your healing for our broken hearts, but slow to extend it to others; we are impatient to demand your release from whatever holds us captive, but reluctant to proclaim release for our neighbors; we are bold to assert our right to the satisfaction of our material needs, but content to spiritualize the needs of others. We dismiss the critics who equate the church with the noise of our solemn assemblies, but we do not provide them with much evidence to the contrary. We do not hesitate to call ourselves the body of Christ, but we do hesitate to embrace Christ's mission. For this, O God, we acknowledge our sin against you, against our neighbors, and against ourselves. And we pray that, just as you come to us at our point of need, you will send us to others at their point of need.

Set us on a course that will lead us to discover gifts we never knew we had and to use them in behalf of people we never knew were there: the poor, the bound, the afflicted, the oppressed, the homeless, the help-less, and the hopeless—the very people in whose service Jesus found the key to his mission and ours. Deliver us from the paternalism that permits us to think less highly of them than we ought. And save us from the individualism that allows us never to think of them at all. As your spirit indwelled the body of the man from Nazareth, let it now indwell your body of believers, so that, when one member rejoices, all will rejoice; when one member suffers, all will suffer; and when one member slips, all will jump to the rescue.

O God, who sent Christ to be the light of the world and the light for the world, shine within us, upon us, around us. When we ignore the people Christ came to serve, illumine our hearts, lest we mistake our selfishness for your indifference. When we ignore the prophets you send to speak, illumine our minds, lest we apply yesterday's solutions to today's problems. When we ignore the commandments you deliver to inspire, illumine our wills, lest we substitute correct ideas for con-structive action. Let all who walk in darkness behold in Christ's body of believers the same light that others who walked in darkness beheld in Jesus.

❧ *Fourth Sunday After Epiphany.* Gracious God, our Lord and Savior, we turn to you in grateful confidence, for you are no stranger to us. Were it not for you, you *could* be a stranger. We do our best to put distance between you and ourselves, but you are better at bringing us together than we are at keeping us apart. You confront us with a power we cannot manipulate, a goodness we cannot match, a love we cannot deny; for this, dear Lord, we bless you and pray for your blessing upon us. Let your power become to us not merely an object of awe but a source of renewal; let your goodness become to us not merely a thing of envy but a model for life; let your love become to us not merely an inescapable force but a contagious presence, that we might remember not only to whom we should give thanks, but why.

We voice this plea, O Lord, with hesitation. Not that we doubt your intentions or your ability to accomplish them. We know that, before we move in love toward you, you have already moved in love toward us; before we seek you, you have already sought us. Nevertheless, we do hesitate, for we are saddled with memories—vivid memories, bitter memories—of the times we failed to conform our action to your intention: when those in life's quicksand might have been rescued, but we did not extend a helping hand; when the cause of justice might have been advanced, but we did not plead its case; when the obstacles to a healthful environment might have been removed, but we did not lend our strength. We would like to forget: the times you said to pluck up, and we continued to plant; the times you said to go here, and we went there; the times you said to do this, and we did that; the times you said to speak boldly, and we spoke timidly, if at all.

When we review these times, we are astounded, O Lord, that you remain near to hear us and to receive us and to forgive us; that you stand ready, even though we repeatedly make you our second choice, to offer us a second chance. So we approach you in repentance and hope, chastened by your ability to remember, yet encouraged by your readiness to forget.

O God, turn our eyes from our unalterable past to our open future: from the hateful words we have spoken to the healing words we yet can speak; from the thoughtless deeds we have done to the thoughtful deeds we yet can do; from the worthless causes we have supported to the worthwhile causes we yet can support; from the uncaring society we have shaped to the caring society we yet can shape.

O Lord, the world is full of people we yet can help. Open our eyes, that we might see them; our hearts, that we might love them; our mouths, that we might defend them; and our hands, that we might assist them, as together we seek to discern and do your will, through Jesus Christ our Lord.

✤ *Fifth Sunday After Epiphany.* Almighty and gracious God, who towers over us with such majesty that we cannot but acknowledge our insignificance, and yet who draws close to us with such mercy that we cannot *deny* our *significance,* we adore you. We adore you for who and what you are. And we thank you for who and what *we* are—and for who and what we can become.

We are grateful, O Lord, for your self-disclosure in Jesus of Nazareth—not because he was so unlike us, but because he was so like you: so like you that we could look at him and see you, we could listen to him and hear you; so like you that we could read his mind and know yours, we could learn his will and obey yours. Yes, Lord, we thank you for Jesus Christ, the revealer of you to us and of us to you.

We also thank you for all those who keep the vision of him vivid and the spirit of him vital: those who, launching their search for you, study his journey with you; those who, seeking your will for them, ponder your guidance of him; those who, confronting the snares of temptation, examine his rebuke of the Tempter; those who, living in the shadow of suffering, remember his victory over Calvary. We owe such a great debt to these people that we can never repay it. Yet we can live and labor, as did they, to reclaim the vision and revive the spirit of Jesus Christ.

For this to happen, O God, the story of our lives must take a new direction. Our story has been of peaks and valleys, with too many valleys and too few peaks. Again and again you have called us to take the high ground, but found us content to settle for the low ground: more anxious to keep the friendship of the privileged than to secure the rights of the disadvantaged; more ready to appease the mighty than to applaud the merciful; more willing, in the struggle for justice, to sit on the sidelines than to stand in the frontlines; more concerned to guarantee the fortunes of our people than to enrich the future of your people; more disposed to claim your support of our causes than to risk our support of your cause.

As we review this story, we bow in shame and in hope—in shame, knowing that we could have written a different story; yet in hope, knowing that, as we write its new chapters, we can count on your help. We pray, dear Lord, that you will make the story of our lives not only different but better—a story of which neither you nor we need be ashamed.

Like Paul, we are among the untimely born. Nevertheless, we pray that you will enable us, like him, to perceive and to mediate the presence of Christ. Deliver us from all the habits of mind and heart and conduct that might hide Christ from our neighbors. Grant us the grace so to represent Christ that his appearances will continue without end.

❧ *Sixth Sunday After Epiphany.*   Gracious Lord and Savior, whose spirit guided Jesus in life and glorified him in death, we adore you for coming to us in him and for leading us to you through him.

As the time between his life and ours grows longer, we are forced to turn to others for our knowledge of him: to the shapers of the traditions about him; the collectors of the stories about his life and teaching; and the commentators who, through the centuries, have related the Lord of the ages to the needs of the age. Often these guardians of the faith have kept it alive and relevant at great personal sacrifice and risk. To them we owe a debt of endless appreciation and gratitude.

And not only to them do we owe this debt, but also to those in whose lives we have beheld the likeness of Jesus. Their names may not be found on the covers of books or even on the pages between. Yet they are the people who come to mind when we ask what Jesus would do in our situation; what you would have us do at a given moment; whether we should take this side or that; how we can most usefully invest our energies and abilities. All of us have known them, and just now, O God, we pay tribute to the beauty of their lives and the influence of their lives on ours. By their example, they have taught us afresh what it means for the Word to become flesh.

Yet our appreciation of them is blunted by the painful awareness of how often we ignore their wise counsel; how rarely we follow their good example; how little we treasure their low regard for things; how casually we dismiss their genuine respect for persons; how lightly we take their unswerving commitment to personal integrity; how easily we betray their passion for social justice.

We cannot undo the mistakes of the past, O God, but you can spare us their repetition. Make clear to us when we are putting our trust in persons who do not put their trust in you. Try our hearts, lest we substitute loyalty to human beings for loyalty to you. As we look to Jesus, through whom you made yourself real to those who made Jesus real for us, grant us the grace to follow in their footsteps. Help us to become to others what they have become to us: prophets of peace and apostles of justice.

✤ *Seventh Sunday After Epiphany.* Gracious God, who endows earthly inhabitants with heavenly dreams and tests mortal limits with immortal longings, you never cease to amaze and confound us. You make life possible, but you also make life unpredictable. For while you create us in your image, filling us with aspirations that only you can satisfy, you grant us our freedom, confronting us with choices that only we can make. You make us creatures of dignity, and you treat us accordingly. You initiate a covenant with us, but you leave it unsealed until we accept it in faith. You could win our acceptance by coercion, but you seek it by choice. You do not rely on the manipulation of your awesome might but on the manifestation of your suffering love; not on superior strength but on amazing grace; not on the power to inflict pain upon us but on the power to endure pain for us. So we thank you, dear Lord, not only for being the God whose image we behold in Jesus, but for being the God who, in Jesus, beholds our image.

O God, who in Christ calls us to conform our lives to your will, we acknowledge our failure to heed this summons. Time and again, even though mindful of his ways, we have not walked in Christ's steps. We knew of his readiness to help those who could not help him, yet we have restricted our help to those who can help us. We knew of his willingness to give to those who could not give to him, yet we have given only to those who can give to us. We knew of his quickness to forgive his enemies, yet we have been slow to forgive even our friends. Forgive us, dear Lord, for our betrayal of your summons. Draw us nearer to yourself, that we might find the desire to discern your will and the strength to do it.

O Lord, as we behold spirited multitudes emerging from long years of bleak oppression, help us to surround them with your spirit; to reassure them of your love and of our readiness, as your agents, to assist them in their struggle for freedom with dignity, order with justice, and peace with honor.

A tumult of voices is calling us, Lord, but only yours is calling us to give hope to the hopeless, help to the helpless, comfort to the friendless, and meaning to the aimless. Help us, amidst all these voices, not only to distinguish yours from all others, but also to heed yours above all others.

❧ *Eighth Sunday After Epiphany.* O God, who has made us in your image, so that we cannot know the life you intend for us until you live in us and we in you, we thank you for the gift of life. We thank you for our life as human beings, the life that sets us apart from all the rest of your creation. We thank you for our life as people of the covenant, the life that sets us apart as your agents for the restoration of all creation. We thank you for our life as members of the body of Christ, the life that sets us apart for the sharing of life as you mean it to be.

Thanks to Jesus Christ, we seek you with knowledge of who you are. Not only has he taught us that we must think your thoughts; he has thought your thoughts. Not only has he taught us that we must feel your feelings; he has felt your feelings. Not only has he taught us that we must do your deeds; he has done your deeds. We do not know you as you know us, but thanks be to Jesus Christ, we know you too well to excuse ourselves for not being more like you.

And we know you too well to think that you do not know us for who we are: persons who long to reap the harvest of love but sow the seeds of hate; who aspire to build bridges to peace but beat the paths of discord; who intend to fill the stomachs of the needy but line the pockets of the greedy; who claim to stand for the cause of justice but bow before the wave of injustice. O Lord, we confess before you and before the world that we are not the people we would like to be, nor the people you would have us be. But where there is life, there is hope, and we are yet alive. And where there is Christ, there is redemption, and Christ is forever among us.

We pray, O God, that, as you have given Christ a glorious body, immortal and imperishable, you will confirm our membership in that body. As he thought your thoughts until he could feel your feelings and do your deeds, enable us to think his thoughts until *we* can feel *his* feelings and do *his* deeds. Deliver us from the self-defeating notion that you cannot work the same works, and even greater works, through his body of believers that you wrought through his body of flesh and blood. Let us not forget that the same spirit that animated his earthly body is alive and at work in his new body, seeking to emancipate us from our past and stamp your claim on our future.

We think now of all those who turn to us in search of you. As the moisture of the heavens nourishes the plants of the earth, let your word bring to glorious harvest the seeds of truth and righteousness in our lives. Help us to confront our neighbors with a harmony between word and deed that inspires confidence. If we impress them, let it be not with the words of our lips but with the works of our lives; not with our holy rhetoric but with our humble resolve; not with our splendid acts of worship but with our gentle acts of mercy. O Lord, let them remember, and let us not forget, that it is for their sake, not our own, that we are sanctified.

❦ *Last Sunday After Epiphany (Transfiguration Sunday).* Gracious God, who knows our weaknesses before we indulge them and meets our needs before we voice them, you are a great and mighty God, Ruler of rulers and Lord of lords. When we consider the distance between us—between you, the only truly Holy One, and ourselves, the very truly human ones—we should be traumatized by fear and reduced to silence. Yet we are not consumed by fear, and we dare to open our mouths as well as our hearts. We enter your presence with joy and thanksgiving, and we speak our minds with confidence and boldness. We approach you not because of who we are, but because of who you are; not because of what we do for you, but because of what you do for us; not because of the obedience with which we serve you, but because of the love with which you seek us.

So we come before you, O Lord, secure in the faith that, even though we deserve abandonment, you will never abandon us; that even though we can never merit your love, you will always love us. You will never stop trying to make us worthy of your adoration, to incline our hearts to your will, to set our feet on the path to peace and justice. For this love—a love that demands obedience, yet woos the disobedient—we are grateful, and by this love we are humbled.

Indeed, when we consider its cost, we are humiliated. We see your love walking the shores of Galilee, speaking comforting words to the lowly, only to be met by indignant cries from the mighty. We see your love moving into a ditch beside the Jericho road, rescuing the victim of highway robbery, only to be chastised for risking travel in a dangerous land. We see your love chatting with a Samaritan woman, aware of her transgressions yet not condemning her, only to be censored by the pious for moral indifference.

Yes, Lord, we are humiliated by your love, for we help to drive up its cost. When the lowly are comforted, we are as apt to speak words of indignation as of approval; when the victims of crime are aided, we are as apt to defend the cautious as to applaud the compassionate; and when sinners are transformed by the love of their neighbors, we are as apt to condemn the neighbors for the company they kept as to commend the sinners for the change they made. Forgive us, O God, for claiming for ourselves a grace that we deny to others. Deliver us from

145

the hypocrisy of our ways, that they who look to us for compassion shall no longer turn from us in frustration.

Gracious God, who in Jesus Christ has commended yourself to us, enable us so to walk among our neighbors that we shall commend Jesus Christ to them. Let us remember, when they turn to us, to direct them to your Chosen, the one of whom you say, "This is my Son; listen to him!"

Lenten Season

❦ *Ash Wednesday.* O Lord, you have appeared among us, but we have not seen you. You have walked among us, but we have not followed you. You have spoken among us, but we have not understood you. You have rejoiced among us, but we have not embraced you.[11] You have suffered among us, but we have not saved you.

We looked for your coming for so long, O Lord! But, with our eyes fastened on the horizon, we missed your approach—until now. Now we see that your day is near, near and hastening fast: a day of distress and anguish, a day of ruin and devastation, a day of clouds and gloom; a day when we shall grope in the blindness of our sin, and our silver and gold shall fail us.[12]

Now, O Lord, we see that your day is near! The earth mourns and withers, and the heavens languish with her. The earth lies polluted beneath us, a curse devours her; she is utterly broken, rent asunder. Staggering under her burdens like a drunkard, she collapses and will not rise again.[13]

Now, O Lord, we see that your day is near! And how we tremble in repentance, we who have violated heaven and earth, who suffer for their pain! How we long for your abundant mercy! Appear again among us, and this time we will see. Walk again among us, and this time we will follow. Speak again among us, and this time we will understand. Rejoice again among us, and this time we will embrace you. Save us from our sin, and you will never suffer again!

Create in us a clean heart, O God, and put a new and right spirit within us. Grant us the mind that was in Christ,[14] and we who have walked in darkness will behold a great light; we who have dwelled in a land of deep shadows, on us shall a light shine.[15] And your people shall say on that day, "Lo, this is the Lord for whom we have waited; let us rejoice in our salvation."[16]

That day can be *this* day, O Lord! So much we know, so little we trust! Give us the courage to turn about and return to you. Deliver us from our vanity, that we might give our gifts and pray our prayers not for recognition, but out of gratitude. Deliver

---

11. See Matthew 11:16-19.
12. See Zephaniah 1:14-18.
13. See Isaiah 24:4-5.
14. See Philippians 2:5-6.
15. Inspired by Isaiah 9:2.
16. See Isaiah 25:9.

us, that we might fast the fast that *you* desire: the fast that will loose the bonds of wickedness and let the oppressed go free; the fast that will break its bread with the hungry and offer its house to the homeless; the fast that will refuse to hide its face from any brother or sister in need.

O Lord, give us the courage to turn about and return to you, and we will return to our neighbor. Then shall your light break forth like the dawn,[17] your grace ascending like the rising sun, and your mercy, as its ray.

🍁 *First Sunday in Lent.*   O God, in whose service we find our freedom, we call upon your name with gratitude for the past and with hope for the future. Words of faith are upon our lips; songs of faith are upon our hearts. The words tell of your righteousness; the songs rejoice in your salvation. For you are the God of our ancestors, of our mothers and fathers who went down into Egypt and were enslaved by the hand of Pharaoh; who cried out to you in the land of Goshen and were heard, for you saw their affliction, their toil, their oppression, and delivered them into a land of milk and honey.

And you are the God of our savior, our brother Jesus, who with his parents went down into Egypt and was saved from the hand of Herod; who cried out to you in the Garden of Gethsemane and was heard, for you saw his torment, his struggle, his sorrow, and brought him into the kingdom of bread and wine.

We are grateful, Lord; for as we retell the story of your righteousness, we participate in that saving history and make it our hope. And our need for that hope is no less than in the past. Temptation creeps into the midst of our salvation. Our parents, having been led into the wilderness by your hand, wandered for forty years, and were sorely tempted; indeed, while you communed with Moses on Mount Sinai, they created a golden calf and proclaimed it god. And our brother, having been led into the wilderness by your Spirit, was tempted for forty days; and when every temptation was ended, his adversary departed only *until a more opportune time.*

The voice of the tempter taunts us, even as it taunted Jesus: *If* you are children of God, turn the stones to bread, and your hunger shall be satisfied! *If* you are children of God, seize the glory of power, and the world shall be yours! *If* you are children of God, throw yourselves off the roof of the temple, and you shall not be hurt! The

17. See Isaiah 58:6-9.

voice seduces us, Lord, sounding like yours. So we live and die, try-ing to turn stones into bread, turning what we want into what we need, and believing, if we get it, that *you* have made it possible. We live and die, climbing the mountain, looking for more power than we have, and believing, if we find it, that *you* have made it happen. We live and die, leaping off the rooftops of our religion, testing the angels of your will, and believing, if we are rescued, that *you* have made it so.

O Lord, how little we comprehend the profanity of trying to tempt you! How little we understand the blasphemy of courting you, as if you could be won or lost; the blasphemy of negotiating with you, as if you could be bought or sold; the blasphemy of examining you, as if you could be judged right or wrong.

O Lord, how we deceive ourselves, believing that you play favorites, forgetting that you are Lord of all; that just as you are the God of the one who cried "Father!" on the cross, you are the God of those who cried "Baal!" before the golden calf; and you are the God of us who cry "Lord, Lord!" and do not do your will.[18]

Forgive us, Lord, for we sin.

Forgive us, Lord, for we would overcome temptation.

Forgive us, Lord, for you alone would we serve—you, in whom alone we find freedom.

🍁 *Second Sunday in Lent.*　O God, in gracious love you promise to care for the creatures of earth; in steadfast love you keep your promise. But we, who so quickly embrace your covenant, just as quickly betray it; we, from whom you desire worship, too often offer only scorn. For making and then keeping your promise in the great-ness of your mercy, we sing your praise, Lord; and for accepting and then spurning your covenant in the greatness of our sin, we ask your forgiveness.

The reality of sin rages furiously in our lives, but the word *sin* sits quietly, often reluctantly, on our lips. Our mouths rebel against its con-fession, against our shame. How little we understand, Lord, that the confession, once spoken, and the shame, once named, can free us from sin—from the power of that which we allow out of fear, honor out of folly, cover by our silence, and cloak with our indifference!

---

18. See Luke 6:46.

You have lit the refiner's fire, Lord;[19] now make glowing embers of our sin. Let the penitent word burn on our tongues, scorching our lips until they are compelled to speak. Let them speak—not that we might grovel in confession, but that we might grow in courage; not that we might take pleasure in humiliation, but that we might receive power in liberation; not that we might wallow in guilt, but that we might rise up in faith.

Forgive us, Lord, for we have sinned.

The word burns, Lord. Let our hearts flame with truth—truth about you, about ourselves, about our neighbors: the truth of how, redeemed by you, we can redeem one another; how, freed by you, we can free one another; how, empowered by you, we can empower one another.

Forgive us, Lord, for we have sinned.

The word burns, Lord. Let our spirits be filled with light—the very Light of the World, the light that shines without blinding, leads without wavering, and glows without ceasing.

Forgive us, Lord, for we have sinned.

The word burns, Lord. Let our bodies dazzle in their transfiguration[20]—in the glory of your in-dwelling, the radiance of your in-spiriting, the brilliance of your in-fleshing.

Forgive us, Lord, for we have sinned.

The word burns, Lord. Let our hands take up the candles of peace—candles whose flame cannot be doused; whose tapers cannot be consumed; whose tallow cannot be melted.

Forgive us, Lord, for we have sinned.

O God, we lift our candles, our lives, to yours. We who so often betray you, embrace you now. We who so often scorn you, worship you now. In the greatness of our sin, we have asked forgiveness. In the greatness of your mercy, you have received us.

❦ *Third Sunday in Lent.*   O God of mercy, we behold a fig tree, and it is without fruit. And we say, "Let us chop it down; why should it use up the ground?" But you say, "No, feed it, and it may live." We approach the tree, curious, cautious, unaware that you convert the ordinary into the extraordinary. And you allow us to come, well aware that we frequently reduce the extraordinary to the ordinary.

---

19. Inspired by Malachi 3:2; Matthew 3:10-12.
20. Inspired by Luke 9:29.

O God of grace, we behold a fig tree dying, and you are not content simply to study us while we study its fruitless branches. You *speak,* and your voice is reassuring, so reassuring that we do not run away but call out, "Here we are!" Yet what you say is at once terrible and wonderful. You reveal yourself to be the God of Abraham and Sarah, of Isaac and Rebecca, of Jacob and Rachel and Leah; the God of Moses and Miriam, of Mary and Joseph, and of Jesus the Christ. You reveal yourself to be the mighty Creator, the eternal beginning and endless end, the infinite sky and bottomless sea, whose life depends on nothing, but whose love gives life to everything.

O God of patience, we behold a fig tree dying, and we hear your voice speaking. We believe you are in our midst, but we are not relieved. Your presence is demanding. Who you are asserts that the world cannot remain as it is, that it must become something new. But change does not come as easily as our protests. "Let the wicked forsake their way, and I will abundantly pardon," you shout. And we object, "What if we are tempted beyond our strength?" I am faithful, and I will give you strength," you cry. Still we complain, "What if we are unable to endure? Why should the risk be ours?" Another time, Lord; another place. Another way, Lord; another face.

O God of love, we see, and hear, and protest, but your purpose will not be thwarted. Pry open our eyes with a barren fig tree; make us see what you see—the deliverance of your people from the threat of death. Unstop our ears with its rustling branches; make us hear what you hear—the cry of the world's oppressed. If your fig tree be barren, let it not be consumed. If its twigs be leafless, let them not be lifeless. Convert the barren into the fruit-bearing, that common people might become uncommon prophets, receivers of new life from you, givers of new life to the world.

🍁 *Fourth Sunday in Lent.*   O Lord, in you our souls make their boast. You are the God who frees the captive, who bears for them the burdens too great, and breaks for them the yokes too heavy, and suffers for them the wounds too grave. You are the God who strengthens the weak, who supports them against winds too strong, and shores them up in struggles too grim, and sustains them down roads too long. You are the God who renews the faint, who swims for them the waters too deep, and leaps for them the hurdles too high, and lights for them the ways too dark.

Stretch out your hand, O Lord, and we will flee the place of our oppression to follow you through the wilderness. Feed us with quail from the sky and manna from heaven; draw water from the rock for our thirst. And it will come to pass that we will need the quail and manna no longer. We will partake of the fruit of the land, of the fruit of our labors, of the harvest reaped by the hands of your people.

Yes, in you, O Lord, our souls make their boast, for in you they will be freed! They bless you at all times, for in you they will be strengthened! They exalt your name together, for in you they will be renewed!

Stretch out your hand, O God, and a new Moses will appear among us as we toil, summoning us to follow. Let him feed us with loaves and fishes; let him turn water into wine for our thirst. And it will come to pass that we will need the loaves and fishes no longer. We will partake of the bread of the kingdom, of the bread of life, of the loaf offered up by the hands of the savior!

Yes, in you, O Christ, our souls make their boast, for in you they will be freed! They bless you at all times, for in you they will be strengthened! They exalt your name together, for in you they will be renewed!

Stretch out your hand, O God, and a new spirit will descend upon us as we wait, to send us into the world. Let her feed us with milk, and the milk will satisfy our hunger and our thirst. But it will come to pass that we will need milk no longer. We will partake of solid food, of the food of prophets, of the feast prepared by the hands of an angel![21]

Yes, in you, O Spirit, our souls make their boast, for in you they will be freed! They bless you at all times, for in you they will be strengthened! They exalt your name together, for in you they will be renewed!

✤ *Fifth Sunday in Lent.*   O eternal God, how often we worship you and how little we understand you:

You, who makes the first to be last and the last to be first;
You, who frees the slave and enslaves the free;
You, who makes wealth to be poverty and poverty, wealth;
You, who chides the pious and feasts with the faithless;
You, who makes foe to be friend and friend to be foe;
You, who brings the outsider in and turns the insider out;
You, who makes success to be failure and failure, success—
You are the God who calls us—a right-side-up people—to become

---

21. Inspired by I Corinthians 3:2; Hebrews 5:12-14; Revelation 10:8-9.

your upside-down kingdom. You call us to be embodiments of a revolution in values, a revolution in which the power of love deposes the
glory of our ambition, in which the freedom of grace breaks our
bondage to greed. How you would love us, how you would save us—
by changing us, by changing our world!

We must ask your forgiveness, Lord. For though you desire our
conversion to a different world, we would rather preserve the world
as it is. Though you desire us to defend the least among us, we
would rather admire the greatest. Though you desire us to serve you
faithfully at all times and in all places, we would rather confine our
faith to the services in our sanctuaries. Though you desire us to
become your upside-down people, we would rather climb the ladder
of right-side-up living.

If only we could say with Paul that we count all gain as loss for your
sake.[22] If only we could offer all that we have, and all that we are, in the
service of all that you would have us become. If only we could realize
that to be baptized is to be turned around, transformed, transfigured; to
be made a new creature, with new eyes to see rightly, new ears to hear
wisely, new lips to speak truly, new minds to think clearly, new hearts
to love greatly; to begin to discern what *right* and *wise* and *true* and
clear and *great* might mean, in the life of radical faith.

If only!

We confess our difficulty in discerning your values, Lord. When
your revelation comes, it is neither easily perceived nor wholeheartedly
received. Even when Christ appears, revealing your values in body and
soul, we cannot agree upon his identity. We hesitate to recognize him,
refuse to acknowledge him: His words are too harsh, his ways are too
hard. He is one of us, yet so unlike us; he offends and confronts, he dis-
rupts and disputes, he defies and demands, and he loves—Great God,
how he loves! Such scandal, this love for sinners! Such shame, this
love for enemies! Such disgrace, this love for outcasts!

If only!

O Lord, stand our values on their head, if they are not also your values. We are capable of becoming upside-down for your sake, but we
are not strong. Send your spirit into our very bones, into the sinew of
our flesh, into the substance of our souls; make us burn with the fire of
compassion, with the flame of conviction, with the light of zeal!

---

22. See Philippians 3:7.

Then we shall understand you whom we worship, and we shall begin
to be what we have begun to understand:
We will make first to be last and last to be first;
We will free the slave and enslave the free;
We will make wealth to be poverty and poverty, wealth;
We will chide the pious and feast with the faithless;
We will make foe to be friend and friend to be foe;
We will bring the outsider in and turn the insider out;
We will make success to be failure and failure, success—
We will be your upside-down people, the embodiments of your revo-
lution in values. And, oh, how we will love you! How we will serve
you—by changing ourselves, by changing our world!

❧ *Passion/Palm Sunday.*   O God, your servant—our Christ—
comes among us this day, and we join the multitudes who celebrate his
coming. We adorn his head with the crown of our hope, we cloak his
shoulders with the robe of our joy. He sits astride a colt never ridden,
but it is the power of our expectations that really carries him into our
midst. He knows our expectations better than we; they taunt him with a
seductive voice, tempting him to be someone you have not meant him
to be, someone you have not sent him to be.

O Lord, little do we understand that, in the space of a week, our
songs of praise will turn into shouts of ridicule; or that we will replace
the crown of hope with one of thorns, and the robe of joy with one of
mockery. Little do we understand that, in the space of a week, this
Jesus will fall from glory to shame; that his eye will waste from grief,
and his life be spent with sorrow; that his strength will fail because of
his misery, and his bones will waste away. Why must he become the
scorn of his enemies, a horror to his neighbors, an object of dread to his
friends? Why must he listen to our whispers as we scheme together
against him, as we plot to take his life, until he is made a broken jar,
crushed in the dirt beneath our heel?

Why, Lord? We understand little, for we do not understand ourselves. You sent this God-man to serve us, to save us, that we might
learn to serve others, to save others. But, caught up in mighty dreams
and changing times, we have not served even *him*. Instead, we have
sought to control him, disciples rising above their teacher. Forgive
us, Lord, for while we have stood waving our palm branches, we
have wondered how supporting him might be to our benefit, how

using him might be to our advantage. Forgive us, for when he has spoken, we have listened for the right words, the easy words, words we have wanted him to speak; and when he has acted, we have watched for the right deeds, easy deeds, deeds we have wanted him to do. Can we, who have not genuinely served him, really be expected to save him?

O God, hear our confession: More than any change for which we yearn, we need a change in mind. Inspire in us the mind that is in Christ, who humbles himself and is obedient, who will be faithful to your will even unto death, even unto death on a hateful cross. If we are too proud to follow him, cast out our vanity, and let us become modest disciples. If we are too angry to follow him, dispel our hostility, and let us become makers of peace. If we are too hesitant to follow him, exorcise our fear, and let us become bearers of courage. Help us to follow him as faithfully as he has followed you, Lord, and we will serve others as he has served us; we will save others, as he has saved us, and we will rescue his life from the traps we ourselves have laid.

❉ *Holy Thursday.*   O God, this Last Supper awakens memories of a Passover when, instead of a man, there was a boy; instead of a teacher among disciples in an upper room, there was a youth among teachers in the temple; instead of a lifted cup and a broken loaf, there was a question risked and an answer dared; instead of a haughty boast from his companions, there was only an air of wonder.

How far Jesus has journeyed between these Passovers! And how far we have walked with him, O God, not to understand! But this night, the hour has come. We sit at table, and Jesus takes a cup, saying, "Take this, and divide it among yourselves." And he takes the bread and breaks it, and gives it to us, saying, "This is my body; do this in remembrance of me." We listen and we watch, but we do not understand. We pass the cup with trembling hands; we pass the bread with lowered eyes.

Lord, we remember the mountain where he taught us, saying, "Blessed are those who hunger and thirst for righteousness, for they shall be satisfied." Satisfied—as the wedding party was satisfied by water turned to wine, as the five thousand were satisfied by a few loaves and fishes.[23] We remember, but we do not understand.

---

23. See Matthew 5:1-2, 6; John 2:1-11; Luke 9:12-17.

Receive the cup and the loaf *in remembrance,* he says. But what is about to happen, O God, that he should become a mere memory? What is yet to come, that his body should be broken and his blood spilled? What is this *new covenant* of which he speaks? What is this *new and living way* he opens?

O Lord, enliven our souls that we might follow his way, enlighten our minds that we might understand his truth, and empower our spirits that we might embody his life. For the *way* of the cup and the loaf is within us; you have written it upon our hearts. And the *truth* of the cup and the loaf is that you shall be our God, and we shall be your people. And the *life* of the cup and the loaf is knowing you—*all* of us knowing you, from the least of us to the greatest.

Make our hearts burn within us,[24] O God. In our communion, transform us; make us a parable of the kingdom and a sign unto the world. If we are caught up in the rapture of our pride, humble us, lest we miss our calling. For Christ anoints us as he was anointed: to preach Good News to the poor, to proclaim release to the captives and recovering of sight to the blind, to set at liberty those who are oppressed and to proclaim the acceptable year of the Lord.[25] Upon *us* Christ confers the mission and the power that we had thought was his alone.

By your love you can save the sinful and make them a sign, O Lord. But if we think our hunger and thirst be already satisfied, Christ's way is not yet our way; his truth is not yet our truth; his life is not yet our life. Though we lift the cup and break the bread with him tonight, tomorrow he shall die alone. We shall forsake him, for we have not yet read what your finger has written upon our hearts.

Forgive us, Lord, for we thought we knew you; forgive us, for we do not know ourselves.

✦ *Good Friday.* O Christ, our Good Shepherd, how fitting that your birth was first announced to shepherds abiding in the fields! Shepherds who hurried to Bethlehem to find you lying in a manger! Shepherds who glorified and praised God for all they had heard and seen! And how fitting that your mother watched silently, pondering in her heart![26]

---

24. See Luke 24:32.
25. Inspired by Luke 4:18-20.
26. See Luke 2:8-20.

Where are the shepherds today, Lord, while your mother's heart is crucified at the foot of your cross?

O Christ, our Wise One, how fitting that your cradle was sought by magi from the East! Magi who followed your star across the sky! Magi who rejoiced and fell down before you, offering their gifts![27] And how fitting that your mother watched silently, wondering in her heart!

Where are the magi today, Lord, while your mother's heart is broken as your robe is gambled away?

O Christ, our Good Teacher, how fitting that you sought the company of teachers, even in your youth! Teachers who sat with you in the temple! Teachers who were amazed at your understanding and astonished by your answers! And how fitting that your mother watched silently, meditating in her heart!

Where are the teachers today, Lord, while your mother's heart is pierced, even as is your side?

Where, indeed, are *we*, O Lord? We who in Nazareth heard you state your mission! We who spoke so well of you, marveling at your gracious words! We who saw you heal the paralytic and were filled with awe! We who witnessed your stilling of the angry winds and waves and were overwhelmed, whispering among ourselves![28] Where, indeed, *are* we?

We who in Jerusalem reveled in your coming, spreading our garments on the road before you—how we blessed you! We who sat at your table in the upper room, breaking the bread and swearing our devotion—how we loved you! We who stood by your side in the garden, brandishing our swords against your enemies—how we would have fought for you!

Where, indeed, are we now, O Lord? Now that you, the Good Shepherd, have become the lamb; now that you, the Wise One, have made foolish the wisdom of the world;[29] now that you, the Good Teacher, have taught the lesson we did not want to learn?

Where are we, indeed, while you deliver your beloved mother and your beloved friend into each other's care?

27. See Matthew 2:1-12.
28. See Luke 4:16-30; 5:17-26; 8:22-26.
29. See I Corinthians 1:20.

Easter Season

❧ *Easter.*   O God, who hears our call before our lips move, who answers our call before it is raised, we praise you for being present among us, for being present *to* us. We praise you especially for being present among us in Jesus Christ, whose life has revealed to us who you are and who we can aspire to become. His life has been truly yours, even while succumbing to the forces of death. And this day he has risen in your glory; he has revealed himself to the women, to those who stayed with him until his terrible end on the cross, and these women have spread the Good News: This Christ is the living Lord of all, even of us, who denied knowing him; and you, O God, are the living God of all, even of us, who crucified him.

This grace of yours, O God—how hard it is to understand, how hard it is to accept! We have mocked the weak and admired the mighty, yet you have loved us—you, who honor the meek and humble the strong. We have abandoned the powerless and tolerated the pitiless, yet you have embraced us—you, who sustain the helpless and subvert the ruthless. Why, O God?

Christ taught us to turn the cheek, and instead we turned away from him. Why have you not turned from us? Christ urged us to call upon your name, and instead we called out for Barabbas. Why have you not called down a curse upon our heads? Christ chose us to proclaim your kingdom, and instead we proclaimed, "We've no king but Caesar!" Why have you not proclaimed, "Enough! No more! You are not my people, and I am not your God"?

We do not understand; the mystery of your grace is too great, too wonderful, too scandalous. But we *accept* this gospel, this Good News, this resurrection—a resurrection not only of the Christ, but of us. *We are become his body!* The stone is rolled away! Unwrap the shroud that confines us, O God, and we shall walk out of this place of death; ours shall be a new life, and we shall walk upon a different earth and under a different sky, where former things are not remembered. Now, if any member of this body suffers, all of us shall suffer together; and if any member of this body rejoices, all of us shall rejoice together.[30]

Christ has risen—we are his body—and all the world rises with us! Glory to you, O God, our savior! Glory to you, for you have hearkened to our unspoken cry and become our salvation, that we might save the

---

30. Inspired by I Corinthians 12:26.

world! Glory to you, for the sound of weeping will no more be heard, and the call of distress will no more be raised! The tomb is empty! Grace has triumphed over the grave, and love is alive! O God, *love us into loving* more and better, that we—the risen body—might bear all things, and believe all things, and hope all things, and endure all things—all of us together! [31]

🍁 *Second Sunday of Easter.* O God, Alpha and Omega, who in Jesus Christ turns the world upside-down, who makes folly of the world's wisdom and wisdom of the world's folly, who mocks the strength of the strong and crowns the weakness of the humble, you are our sovereign and savior, and we adore you.

We thank you, O Lord, for Easter: for the ways it kindles our awareness of who Jesus was and what he was about; of who you are and what you are about; of who we are and what we are about. In Jesus your character and our destiny were joined, and you promised that his work would not end with his death. You kept that promise, dear Lord; not only did the apostles take you at your word, they took your word to the world. And for this we thank you: not only for the favor with which the world responded to them, but for the faith with which they confronted the world.

When we compare our faith with theirs, O God, we are humbled. They were bold; we are timid. They turned the crucifixion into a model for discipleship; we turn discipleship into an alternative to crucifixion. They interpreted Easter as a summons to choose between divine and human rule; we interpret Easter as the divine sanction of human rule. They received the resurrection as a call for radical decision; we receive it as a proof of ultimate security. They identified the suffering servant with the risen Lord; we glorify the risen Lord at the expense of the suffering servant.

Forgive us, O God, for separating Good Friday from Easter: for believing that, because our Lord's Easter lay behind us, no Golgotha lies before us; for supposing that, because he risked everything, we need not risk anything. Forgive us, above all, for thinking that, because we praise him loudly, we need not follow him closely.

We acknowledge, O God, that our divorce of Easter from Good Friday has done us no good and others much harm. Help us to proclaim

---

31. Inspired by I Corinthians 13:7.

the oneness of the empty tomb and the cross, to narrow the gap between our confession and our conduct. Empower us so to live that our works will confirm the words of our Lord about true greatness. Send us into the world, as you sent him into the world, to become the victorious servants of all.

✤ *Third Sunday of Easter.*   O Christ, we had thought you dead: We mourned in hiding, grieving your death and lamenting our loss, fearing a future without you. When finally we emerged from our hiding places, we hurried back to our old routines, our old priorities, our old livelihoods. We were determined to put the past behind us, to forget it like a bad dream. We sacrificed your visions to common sense; we surrendered our ideals to the "real" world. But our labors were empty—until we caught a glimpse of you on the shore, until you instructed us to cast our net on the other side of the boat.

You are our brother, Lord—our brother, our master, our teacher, our friend, you are all these things and more. But, though we spring into the sea and swim to the shore and run to greet you on the beach, you are not convinced of our love. Who would not adore you when their nets are full of fish?

Three times you ask us, "Disciples, do you love me?" Three times we insist, "Lord, you know that we do!" And you can only reply, "Then feed my lambs, and tend my sheep; feed my flock, and follow me."

O risen brother, who breaks bread with us like no one we have ever known, we confess that our love for you has been timid. We have been faithful to you in the good times and faithless in the bad. When we believed you to be dead and buried, the fire died in our souls, and we buried our hopes in a tomb that was deeper and darker than yours, a tomb carved out by our fears. But now your return has rolled the stone away, and all our confidence and conviction and courage stride out into the sunlight, resurrected by the sound of your voice.

We behold you, O Christ, and in the radiance of your presence, we behold how absent has been our faith. Forgive us. We have let living take precedence over loving; we have let self hold sway over neighbor. So you must remind us that the only measure of our regard for the shepherd is our regard for the flock. "If you love me," you repeat, "feed my lambs, tend my sheep, feed my flock, follow me."

O Christ, once you called us to be fishers; now you summon us also to be shepherds. Help us to watch over the flock that you have entrusted to our care—not grudgingly, not because we have to do so, but willingly, because we want to do so.[32] Once you called us to be disciples; now you summon us also to be servants. Help us to serve the ones you have placed in our path—the hungry and the thirsty, the naked and the stranger, the sick and the imprisoned. Help us to open our arms to those we once despised or ignored, to those we once persecuted by what we did or did not do. Help us to bless them, saying, "Come, inherit the kingdom prepared for you from the foundation of the world."[33]

O Lord, we have proclaimed with our lips that you are the Son of God; help us to proclaim with our lives that we are the people of God. With our words we have confessed our love for you; help us, with our deeds, to confess your love for the world.

❀ *Fourth Sunday of Easter.* O Creator God, Breath of the universe and Heartbeat of the earth, you are our beginning and our end and our in-between. You are our salvation—not only on this, but on every day. You are our deliverance—not only for ourselves, but for our neighbor. You are our redemption—not only from our sin, but from those who sin against us.

O God, we need you. We are frail, but your strength makes us strong in our frailty. We are foolish, but your wisdom makes us wise in our folly. We are vain, but your humility makes us humble in our vanity. Your life in us makes us more and better than we are. For this we praise you: not that you stoop to us, but that you lift us up; not that you condescend to care for us, but that you elevate us to care for one another.

This is your way, Lord. This is your truth. And in Christ we see that this is your life. His works, done in your name, bear witness to you. Yet, though we assent to what he says and admire what he does, we do not believe with all our heart and soul and mind and strength. Time and again, we beg for reassurance: "If this one is really the Christ," we say, "tell us plainly." Time and time again, we plead for another sign: "If this one is truly the Christ, show us clearly."

O Lord, forgive us for our disbelief in the presence of such a divine life—of such a human life—as that of Jesus Christ. Understand the greatness of our temptation to opt out of your way, to opt for another

32. See I Peter 5:2.
33. Inspired by Matthew 25:34-35.

truth, to opt into another life. As time passes, the glory of the open grave pales; more and more we remember the shame, the pain of the rugged cross. Our once-certain step falters; our once-constant faith wavers. Can we really drink of the cup? Are we really willing to receive the baptism that was Christ's?[34] Can we really carry our cross? Are we really willing to carry our neighbor's?

·Our temptation is to find another Christ to follow. Though this Christ be yours, though this Christ be risen, we would make him someone else. We would reduce him to a meek and mild savior, who demands nothing from us and gives everything to us; we would tame him, paint him as someone lovely to look at, pleasant to be with, wonderful to sing about.

O God, on Easter the thunder of your voice caused the stone to roll away from Christ's tomb. Now speak again, on behalf of Christ's people! Declare once again that this Christ, your servant and our Savior, has come to establish justice upon the earth.[35] *Justice*—not mere felicity, although he celebrates joy; not mere tolerance, although he celebrates diversity; not mere tranquillity, although he celebrates peace. No, he comes first to establish *justice,* and he shall not be stopped!

Tell it, Lord! Speak to us! Cause the rock of our self-concern to crumble, to tumble into the crevasse of our self-doubt! Make the ground shake beneath us, so that our feet shall dance, so that we shall leap up and run out the door, and carry mercy to a world awaiting its healing! Make the air tremble around us, so that our tongues shall shout, so that we shall sing from the rooftops, and announce Good News to a world awaiting its release!

You can change us in a flash, Lord! in a word! Choose this moment! Give the command! And we will bear witness to you with our works of justice, filling the earth with deeds done in your name!

❧ *Fifth Sunday of Easter.* Almighty God, in Jesus you entered this life in the likeness of a human being and left it in the likeness of a divine being. In him you taught us the meaning of humanity and unveiled the mystery of divinity. In him you removed the sting of sin and shattered the fear of death. We come before you in the name of Christ our Lord, assured that, as we participate in his death to sin, we

---

34. See Mark 10:38-39.
35. See Isaiah 42:1.

shall partake of his life in faith. Teach us, as you taught him, that just as we must live to die, we must die to live. And move us, as you moved the apostles, to interpret life on earth as an infiltration from heaven.

The apostles faced far greater dangers than we face, braved far more powerful enemies, took far more painful risks, and traveled far less friendly roads. Still they nourished the gospel to glorious flower. Can we make such a claim for ourselves, O God? Are our neighbors ever tempted to interpret our life among them as your descent into their midst? They look to us for your works, but sometimes they look in vain: Instead of faithful speech, they find faithless speech; instead of gracious deeds, selfish deeds; instead of support for the fallen, unconcern; instead of deliverance for the oppressed, indifference; instead of bread for the hungry, empty rhetoric; instead of evidence of the Crucified's resurrection, testimony to the resurrection of the crucifiers.

Our witness for Christ has not been as clear as it should have been or as compelling as it could have been. For this, O Lord, we are deeply ashamed and truly sorry. We pray that you will replace our shame with grace and our remorse with mercy; that henceforth, with singleness of purpose and purity of heart, we might bear faithful witness to the gospel and to you.

As we look at our world, we see multitudes of unhappy, discouraged, ill-clad, ill-fed, hungry, thirsty, and desperate people, many of whom are so fed up with the old earth that the best they can hope for is the old heaven. They despair of ever living on an earth where their hunger will be satisfied, their tears wiped away, their thirst quenched, and their longings fulfilled. Nevertheless, this is the new earth to whose creation Christ calls us. Grant us, O God, the compassion to envision such an earth, the will to work for it, and the grace to live on it.

Without price Christ has quenched our thirst with water from the fountain of life. He has shown us what your witnesses must be and what they must do. We pray, dear Lord, that your spirit, the spirit that in Jesus produced the new being, will in us produce the new earth.

🍁 *Sixth Sunday of Easter.*   O Christ, the promise of whom nourished Israel's hope for the future, the life of whom inspired the apostles' mission to the world, the spirit of whom kindles our zeal for your reign, we come before you in gratitude. We thank you for your revelation—your revelation to us of God, and your revelation to us of ourselves. We thank you for making God more lovable and humanity more responsible; for making the law more flexible and duty more personal; for making religion less forbidding and goodness more appealing; for making revelation less a matter of the head and truth more a matter of the heart; for making God less an idea to be learned and more a presence to be experienced.

When we think of all the changes you have wrought, O Christ, we can only marvel at the difference you have made in history and humanity. Yet we are sobered by the even greater difference you *could* make, if only we would not stifle the spirit you let loose in the world—by putting uniformity of belief before unity of spirit; by putting correct doctrine before compassionate deed; by putting holy sacraments before human service; by putting yesterday's tradition before today's revelation; by putting the record of someone else's experience of God before our own experience of God. Forgive us, O Christ, for diminishing your influence. Grant us the grace to entrust our lives to the guidance of your Holy Spirit, that we might not only see your light, but follow.

Your prophets have told us of a great and wonderful city—a city to which darkness never comes, a city whose gates never close, a city in which all nations and peoples are welcome; a city whose Maker and Ruler is God, who governs its inhabitants with justice and judges them with equity. Deliver us from the temptation to dismiss this vision as if it had no relevance. Enable us to receive it as your message and as a pattern for the conduct of our life on earth. Put us in remembrance of your ways, O Christ, and incline our hearts to walk in them. Let us recall how you ministered to people not on the basis of your creed, but on the basis of their need; how you subordinated the demands of conventional piety to the claims of simple decency; how you put the alleviation of human misery ahead of the satisfaction of religious authority; how you spurned the applause of the mighty for service to the masses.

O Christ of God, you are not dead but alive and well. You live and reign over the new Jerusalem, the city in which there is no housing shortage, no unemployment, no lack of access to education or medical care, and food enough to go around. As you have opened its gates and your heart to us, send us forth to open its gates and our hearts to others.

🍁 *Seventh Sunday of Easter.*   Eternal God, whose rule spans the heavens and surrounds the earth, whose power bestows life and conquers death, whose love includes all generations and embraces all peoples, we come before you in the name of Christ our Lord.

You bless us with gifts we have yet to discover and powers we have yet to exercise; you set us in an environment where they can flourish and among neighbors who can help decipher their mystery. We thank you, dear Lord, for the glory and grandeur of our existence and, above all, for Jesus Christ, in whom you confront us with the full development of these gifts and powers: the One who, by being born, brought heaven to earth and, by dying, raised earth to heaven; the One who, when he gave up life in his flesh-and-blood body, resumed life in his body of believers; the One who taught us that, if we would fulfill our human destiny, we must not forget our divine origin.

Yet how easily we forget his teaching! He taught that justice and righteousness are the foundations of your reign, yet our hearts continue to covet power and privilege. He taught that you are a jealous God, yet our idols continue to multiply. He taught that you are the God of all peoples, yet our prejudices continue to destroy us. He taught that you long to give the water of life to all who thirst, yet our greed continues to check its flow. Forgive us, O God, for trimming Christ's teaching to the size of our desires.

If it be that we cannot bear witness to Christ without cost to ourselves, we pray, O Lord, for the grace and strength to pay that cost without complaint or regret. Embolden us, as you did Paul and Silas, when they disturbed an entire city in defiance of Roman law. If, for the sake of your neglected children, you call upon us to disrupt the indifference of the powers that be, let us answer, like prophets, "Here are we, Lord; send us!"[36]

Let us not disturb the world merely for the sake of creating a disturbance, but to hasten the increase of justice and righteousness: by bringing food to the hungry, housing to the homeless, freedom to the oppressed, dignity to the abused, strength to the weak, and hope to the helpless. O God, where there is true peace, *your* peace—peace with justice—help us to keep it; but where there is false peace—peace with injustice—make us bold, for your sake and for the sake of its victims, to sound the prophet's cry for change.

---

36. See Isaiah 6:8.

Season After Pentecost

❦ *Pentecost.* O God, who is present with us in more ways than we can count—turning confusion into order, condemnation into deliverance, and isolation into fellowship—we thank you for all the ways you are present. We especially thank you for taking the initiative in bringing us together: in creation, by stamping your image upon us; in Christ, by manifesting your love for us; and at Pentecost, by sending your spirit upon us. You have spared no effort in your search for us, and for this, O God, we give thanks.

Yet we must plead guilty to not returning the compliment. Not only do we fail to seek you as you seek us, but we run from you after you find us. Instead of turning to you for counsel, we turn to others; instead of looking to Christ for an example, we imitate our neighbors; instead of seeking a common tongue, we multiply the tongues of pride. As a consequence, we are confused persons in the midst of a confused people, speaking not the one tongue of a common love but the many tongues of private ambition, working not to bring humanity together but to keep it apart.

Forgive us, O God, for thus betraying your purpose: for failing to see that we cannot go it alone without going astray; that we can realize your destiny for us only in community; and that the Holy Spirit, which is working to effect our union with you in heaven, is also working to effect our union with our neighbors on earth.

O God, let your spirit descend upon us as it descended upon the crowds in Jerusalem. Let it strike us as a mighty wind, blowing away the chaff of pride. Let it burn within us as a tongue of fire, consuming the dross of selfishness. And let it lead us forth into the world, proclaiming the dawn in which the young see visions and the old dream dreams, and pursuing your mission in a community bent on becoming the body of Christ.

We are your children, O Lord, and joint heirs with Christ to all your gracious gifts. Let us not betray our heritage. As Christ served his heritage by revealing you to others, let us serve ours by revealing him to others. And as his neighbors came to know you through him, let ours come to know him through us.

O God, let us never forget that the church of Jesus Christ is as dependent upon the Spirit for its life as for its birth. It is the Spirit who gives us the faith to envision one world, the motivation to love its peoples, the determination to discern their needs, and the will to serve them in the name of Christ our Savior. So we pray not merely for an increase in the membership of the church, but for the outpouring of your spirit upon its members. Let it come upon us with the power that compels, the truth that convicts, and the love that converts. Let Pentecost cease to be a past to be remembered and become again a present to be experienced.

❧ *Trinity Sunday (First Sunday After Pentecost).* Almighty and eternal God, whose mystery defies our knowledge yet defines our meaning, whose love transcends our understanding yet transforms our existence, and whose power incites our fear yet inspires our faith, we praise your holy name. We pray that you will grant us a fuller vision of yourself and the strength so to live that we shall reveal you as clearly as we see you.

No matter in what direction we look, whether up or down or around or within, the evidence of your handiwork confronts us. No matter what we behold—whether the spacious heavens above us, the good earth beneath us, the teeming creatures around us, or the aspiring person within us—your wisdom overwhelms us. We cannot contemplate anything you have made without standing in awe of its Maker. You are indeed a great and wise God, O Lord, but we adore you for something greater than your greatness and wiser than your wisdom. Above all, we adore you for the love that will not let us go, the love that has pursued us from the time we began to turn a wilderness into civilization until we started turning civilization back into wilderness. It is the love that tells us that, no matter how badly we deface your image, we can never destroy it. It is the love that assures us that, just as the spirit of Christ moved in the church of yesterday, it moves in the church of today.

Yet we must confess, O Lord, that our conduct as often impresses our neighbors with the absence of Christ as with his presence. While applauding his call for peacemaking, we exercise our preference for troublemaking. While praising his outcries against oppressors, we withhold our support for the oppressed. While admiring his union of belief and behavior, we overlook our tendency to separate them. While hailing his demand for compassion, we press our demand for retribution. While commending his practice of thinking with his heart, we indulge our habit of thinking with our spleen.

O God, forgive us for all the ways we contribute to the world's sense of Christ's absence. Pour out your spirit upon us, that his presence might again be felt moving among us, making us whole and making us one. Take from us our estrangement from the poor, the first to whom Christ brought the Good News. Take from us our insensitivity to the brokenhearted, the first to whom Christ brought healing. Take from us our unconcern for the captive, the first to whom Christ brought liberty. Take from us our disdain for the sorrowful, the first to whom Christ brought comfort.

O Lord, come among us now as before. Come among us, as in creation, to stamp your image on all your creatures. Come among us, as in Christ, to offer your love to your creatures gone wrong. Come among us, as at Pentecost, to breathe your blessing upon your creatures united in fellowship, that we might be encouraged by one another's faith.[37]

❧ *Sunday Between May 29 and June 4 (if After Trinity Sunday).*   Eternal God, who in Jesus Christ redeems us from the sin that drives us apart and reconciles us with the love that brings us together, we thank you for him who has made us your partners in covenant. We bless you for the vision with which you bless us through him: for the vision of yourself, whose love for all does not diminish your love for each; for the vision of us as individuals, whose move away from you does not slow your move toward us; for the vision of the community of believers, whose history of division does not alter your desire for union; and for the vision of the world, whose clamor for power does not silence your demand for justice.

O God, grant us the faith of Solomon's prayer: the faith that calls the temple not by the builder's name but by your name; the faith that looks not within the temple but beyond for your dwelling place; the faith that longs for the temple to become a house of prayer—not for one people but for all the peoples of the earth.

Unfortunately, our faith in Christ has often been no match for Solomon's prayer. We sing of Christ for all the world, but the world we have in mind is much smaller than the world for which Solomon prayed. It is not the world of "all the peoples of the earth," but only some of them—those of them who think as we think, feel as we feel, worship as we worship, and live as we live.

Forgive us, O God, not only for shrinking your world to the size of our prejudices, but for reducing Christ to the level of our preferences.

---

37. See Romans 1:12.

Too often we turn your Christ into a Christ of our own creation: a Christ too narrow to tolerate any behavior we do not approve; to sanction any belief we do not hold; to welcome any person we do not like; to permit any worship we do not practice.

O God, you have made us in your image. Forgive us for remaking the world in ours. You have made Christ the church's one foundation. Forgive us for trying to build it on another. Transform us, O Lord. Grant us the grace so to represent the Christ you have sent that the world might receive your glorious gospel, obey your great commandments, and worship your holy name.

❋ *Sunday Between June 5 and June 11 (if After Trinity Sunday).*   O God of glory and God of grace, whose majesty adorns the heavens and whose mercy fills the earth, who needs nothing we can give yet gives us everything we need, who silences the shouts of the proud yet amplifies the whispers of the humble, we come before you in awe and gratitude. We stand in awe of the glory with which you bless the universe; we bow in gratitude for the light with which you illumine our life.

When we ponder the awful power of nature—the winds of the tornado, the waves of the hurricane, the rumblings of the earthquake—we are reminded not only of your incredible might but of our incredible weakness. In the face of such power, we are helpless. But once nature's fury has subsided and her face is again creased with a smile, we are struck not only by your incredible gentleness but by our incredible strength.

O Lord, we do not know whether the day will come when we can fully harness the power of nature. Yet we can surely understand it better, so that we are able to reduce its capacity for destruction. Quicken our thirst for such understanding, but deliver us from the temptation to dwell only upon nature's power for destruction. Let us celebrate her power for blessing and her potential for healing.

We thank you, O Lord, for the healing power of nature. Help us to bring those in need of healing within her reach. You have given us not only enough fertile land to produce goods adequate for the human family, but the science of agriculture for increasing the supply. Help us to use this science for the sake of your children. You have given us not only enough food to eliminate hunger, but the science of nutrition for maximizing its benefits. Help us to use this science for the sake of your children. You have given us not only antidotes to attack disease, but the science of medicine for spreading health. Help us to use this science for the sake of your children.

O God, we are grateful for the healing power you mediate through nature. We are even more grateful for the healing presence you mediate through people: through those who speak a comforting word in times of mourning; those who lend a helping hand in times of suffering; those who play a supporting role in times of loneliness; those who offer a saving loan in times of need; those who suggest a clarifying course in times of confusion. Join our resources to yours, and make us mediators of your healing presence, that the world might praise you all the day, every day.

🍁 *Sunday Between June 12 and June 18 (if After Trinity Sunday).* Gracious God, into whose presence we come with confidence because you come to us in grace, we pause now, as pilgrims on a journey, for renewal and direction. Others have offered us water for our thirst, but it is not quenched; food for our hunger, but it is not satisfied; a map for our guidance, but it is not clear. So now we come unto you, for you have the water that can quench our thirst, and we know that you will give us to drink; you have the food that can satisfy our hunger, and we know that you will give us to eat; you have the map that can help us find the way home, and we know that you will give us to see.

We thank you, dear Lord, not only for the gifts with which you bless us, but for the welcome with which you greet us. Just as your gifts tell us that you are glad to be our host, your welcome tells us that you are ready to be our guide; and this is what we pilgrims of the way desire above all else.

Yet we turn from you more often than we return to you. Although our meetings with you never fail to renew us, they take place all too rarely. We allow them to become spasmodic and occasional. We long for you, not as those who exult in your name, but as the addict for a quick fix; not as the pioneer for a new homeland, but as the traveler for overnight accommodation; not as the truth-seeker for wisdom, but as the novelty-hunter for entertainment. When you ask, "Why have you forgotten me, O my people?" we answer, "Why, O Lord, have you forgotten *us?* Why do many of us, who love and worship you, fare less well than many who do not? Does our piety count for nothing? Are our prayers and presence in this place of no consequence?"

Teach us, dear Lord, that you call us not for our glorification but for yours. Teach us that you sanctify us not for our sake but for the sake of our neighbors. Awaken us to our brothers and sisters, for whose fulfillment you anoint us as your servants. Let us not envy them if you love them before they deserve it, lest we forget that you love us before *we* deserve it.

We thank you, O God, for reminding us how much we are like others. And we thank you, even more, for reminding us how important others are to you: how you love them as deeply as you love us; how you long for them to become one—not only with us but with you. Let us tarry no longer. Enlist us now, dear Lord, as co-laborers with you in breaking down the dividing walls of hostility, whether between them and us or between ourselves and you.

❧ *Sunday Between June 19 and June 25 (if After Trinity Sunday).* O God of awesome power and disquieting silence, we bow in adoration before you, grateful for the loud thunder that removes you far from us and for the gentle whisper that draws you close to us. Through the ages you have come to us in tones that muffled the sound of your presence, in visions that dimmed the sight of your appearance, and in forms that defied the touch of your being. Yet we continue to look for you, as did Elijah, in the rushing wind, the trembling earth, and the streaking fire, but we are disappointed until we stop looking and learn to listen: until we stop looking for your cosmic fireworks and learn to listen for a gentle whisper.

Help us, O God, to learn how to listen, especially to you. Forgive us for insisting not only on the last word but on the first word; for reporting to you how our neighbors victimize us, as if you were unaware of their transgression; for dictating to you how you can help us, as if you were unaware of our need; for reminding you how often justice is frustrated, as if you were unaware of its miscarriage; for advising you how swift retribution must be, as if our times were not in your hands.

O Lord, forgive our shameless presumption. Not only do we seek to put words in your mouth, but we try to wrench the reins of authority from your hand. We are unwilling to wait for your judgment, preferring to assert our own; unwilling to trust your justice, preferring to administer our own; unwilling to respect your schedule, preferring to set our own. Forgive our impatience, and grant us the humility to stop thinking of ourselves more highly than we should and to start thinking of you as highly as we ought.

O Lord, teach us the beauty of silence, especially in your presence, until we learn the ways of the divine-human dialogue. Break the silence with a word of grace until we join the conversation with an act of faith; until we are ready to grant you the last word; until we recognize that you, and you alone, may set the time for speaking that word.

This we pray, dear God, for the sake of all your children. We will not do right by them until we see them as you see them and esteem them as you esteem them. Deliver us from the temptation to give them what they deserve, rather than what they need. Enable us to go to others in their need as you come to us in ours. As you give yourself for us, let us give ourselves for our neighbors.

❦ *Sunday Between June 26 and July 2.*   O God of gracious word and mighty deed, we thank you for your holy presence. It has been the staff of our life and the source of our faith from the day of our birth, and from generation to generation of all those who have gone before us. When the Israelites threatened to trade you for alien gods, you sent prophets to herald the perils of idolatry. When the powerful began to exploit the weak, you raised up lawgivers to proclaim the demands of justice. Beg as we may to be free of the watchful eye of heaven, you will not leave us alone. We thank you, dear Lord, for your refusal to respect our privacy. We thank you, too, that we are never so fully present to ourselves as when you are fully present to us.

Yet we must confess, O God, that we, like our ancestors, confuse your presence with that of an alien deity. We fill your mouth with words that are less than gracious. We ascribe to you deeds that are less than noble. We turn our enemies into your enemies, putting our sword into your hand. We pillage their land for our own use, crediting you with the transfer of title. We justify your preferential treatment of us, claiming your hatred for them. Shamelessly, we identify our passions with yours, shrinking your compassion to the size of ours.

O God, forgive our indulgence of the works of the flesh that Christ crucified, and for our crucifixion of the works of the spirit that Christ indulged. Let us not forget that the freedom for which Christ set us free is not the freedom through power to become masters but the freedom through love to become servants.

Help us, O God, to become faithful servants—servants who will inspire others to heed your summons without hesitation; servants who will make a difference in the world as in the church. Let us, as when we first believed, put our hand to the plow and, without looking back, use our freedom to multiply the fruits of your spirit.

❀ *Sunday Between July 3 and July 9.*   Gracious God, who withholds from us nothing that we might serve you in everything, we thank you for welcoming us to membership in your family and to partnership in your mission. We thank you, too, that even while denying us equality with your person, you encourage our pursuit of your purpose. And we thank you that you never weary of giving us clues to what that purpose is and how we might advance it.

O God, through your lawgivers and prophets you demonstrated your displeasure with wickedness, boastfulness, deceitfulness, and blood-thirstiness. And when we turned your hatred of evil into a hatred of evildoers, you spoke a corrective word through Jesus, making clear that you seek the destruction not of the sinful but of sin, not of the deceitful but of deceit, not of the violent but of violence.

But we have been slow to understand. We continue to divide the world into hostile camps, one pious and the other profane, one law-observing and the other law-breaking, one faithful and the other faith-less, one humble and the other proud. Ignoring Christ's reminder that he came to call not the well but the sinful to repentance, we identify ourselves as the well and others as the sinful, dehumanizing them and echoing the psalmist's cry for their punishment. We dismiss them as if you could not redeem them; we treat them as if you did not create them.

O Lord, how we wish that we had had nothing to do with the sowing of what we are reaping! But we were there when the seeds of smug superiority were scattered among the underprivileged, the underfed, and the undervalued. Try as we may, we cannot wash our hands of all blame for the harvest of shame they have produced. We can only pray for the strength to survive this harvest and, once it is past, for the wisdom to sow seed that will yield a very different harvest.

The fields are indeed white unto harvest, O God. The seeds of our bigotry and intolerance and selfishness and indifference have yielded bountiful crops. The laborers in the fields grow faint. We pray, therefore, to the Lord of the harvest: Raise up more laborers to destroy the fruit of this planting, that we might prepare the soil for the next.

❀ *Sunday Between July 10 and July 16.*   O Christ, whose wisdom we try to test with our questions, whose love we try to earn with our works, silence us with a parable, humble us with a miracle! Tell us wondrous stories of Samaritans: of people who dare to touch those whom others have judged untouchable; of people who rise above long-held prejudices to kneel at the side of the wounded; of people who sacrifice time and comfort, and even pride, to save a stranger from pain.

Tell us such miraculous stories, O Christ, that our knowledge of you might increase—you who sacrificed your*self* on a criminal's cross to save your enemies. Help us to understand what you mean by *eternal life,* that we might stop trying to purchase a glorious future with righteous works. Turn our attention away from ourselves, that we might begin living eternally, *here* and *now,* showing mercy to those who are in need of mercy, even as we are shown mercy while yet unmerciful. Help us to stop abandoning to others the fate of the world while seeking privilege for ourselves; help us to begin acknowledging our responsibility to care, before the opportunity to care has passed us by.

Strengthen us in your power, Lord! It is *your* power, united with our weakness, that enables us to love someone besides ourselves. It is your power, united with our weakness, that enables us to be patient with the pain of others. It is your power, united with our weakness, that enables us to rejoice in the relief of suffering, no matter how great the cost.

We give thanks to you, O Christ, that the world has been so ordered that the power of love is the supreme power—that the power of love, even more than a faith that moves mountains, is what turns *no*bodies into *some*bodies. We praise you that what is patient and kind is superior to what is angry or cruel; that what is trusting and humble is superior to what is jealous or boastful; that what is modest and respectful is superior to what is arrogant or rude; that what can bear all things, believe all things, hope all things, and endure all things is superior to what abandons all things, doubts all things, laments all things, and concedes all things.[38]

O Lord, in the power of love we ask you: Bestow upon us a double share of your spirit. You have charged us, "If you love me, you will keep my commandments, caring for your neighbor and serving your God." You have promised us, "If you believe in me, you will do greater works than mine."[39] Dear Christ, you know that we love you; help us to love our neighbor more deeply and our God more surely. Let your spirit

---

38. This paragraph inspired by I Corinthians 13:2, 4-7.
39. Inspired by John 14:15, 12.

descend upon us, and like the Samaritan, we shall pour it out upon a suffering world, that all might be saved according to your tender mercy.

✤ *Sunday Between July 17 and July 23.* O Christ, you enter our community, and we receive you into our house. Sometimes, like Mary, we sit at your feet, listening to your teaching; other times, like Martha, we are distracted with much serving, and we complain that the work has been left to us alone. Then you answer us, saying, "You are anxious and troubled about many things, but only one thing is needed."

Only one thing is needed. How often we forget, Lord, and how often we doubt, that what you most need is not our waiting *upon* you, but our waiting *for* you—waiting for the word, through whom all things are made, and without whom nothing is done.[40] We forget; we doubt, because waiting is not easy for us. We live in a bustling world in the midst of bustling people. We have little patience and much ambition; we have little time and much talk. We fidget in silence. We squirm in idleness. We teach our children that those who say nothing have nothing to say, and that those who hesitate are lost.

O Christ, interrupt our busyness with a word about mindfulness, lest we forget the God who gives us birth. Disrupt our distractedness with a call to attention, lest we forget the Lord who provides for life. Convict us if, when we have eaten and are full, we say in our hearts, "The work of our own hands has satisfied our hunger."[41] Teach us what it means to prepare only our *daily* bread,[42] and then bless and break that loaf together in your presence, that the one loaf might multiply and feed a thousand, and then a thousand thousands.[43]

Convince us, Lord, that one thing is needed for all other things; that waiting for you must come before waiting upon others. Without the word, how shall we know what is to be done, and when, and where, and how! For your word is the *why* of our deeds; it is the truth of our life!

Many things are needed, and many things shall be. We offer ourselves to you fully, O Christ; we are with you without reservation, without distraction. Speak to us, telling us that all things are possible if

---

40. Inspired by John 1:3.
41. Inspired by Deuteronomy 32:18; 8:11-18.
42. See Matthew 6:11.
43. Inspired by Matthew 14:13-21.

only we believe, for all things *are* possible with God. Call to us, inspiring us to the fullness of faith, for faith is nothing, if not the assurance of things hoped for and the conviction of things not seen. And charge us with the living out of the gospel, for the gospel is nothing, if not the promise of all things being made new, through our God and for our neighbor.[44]

🍁 *Sunday Between July 24 and July 30.* O God, whose breath stirs the trees, whose pulse moves the rivers, we praise you for your presence in our world. We can trust your presence—around us, among us, with us, with*in* us—above all else. If shades of light and dark play tricks on our eyes, we can look to you for clarity in seeing. If clamoring voices make fools of our ears, we can listen to you for clarity in hearing. If competing powers make claims on our hearts, we can turn to you for clarity in deciding. Yours is the light beside which all others are dim, the voice before which all others are faint, the power against which all others are weak.

We thank you, dear Lord, that we can take your presence for granted. But let us not take your presence lightly. Let us never forget that your presence makes two demands upon us: that we love you with all our heart and soul and mind and strength, and that we love our neighbors as ourselves—two great demands, which really are but one, like the rising and the setting sun.

Only one commandment . . . why do we have such trouble remembering, Lord? We can fill our minds daily with all kinds of facts and figures, memorize lists of names and lines of poetry, plan for a day twenty years hence or recollect a day twenty years before; but when the facts tell us that someone needs help, when the figures show that someone is in trouble, we cannot remember our responsibility, before them and before you. Forgive us, Lord, when we thus deny our baptism.

We are your people, O God. We would live in Christ! We would be rooted in the goodness of Christ, like the great forests are rooted in the good earth! Yet we are afraid, we pull back. We live in a rapidly changing world, with shifting values and uncertain loyalties. Some of us want to conquer that world with our own schemes and skills and sweat. Others of us want to retreat. Our hands, which you would stretch toward the stricken, we use to cover our ears; our eyes, which you would turn

---

44. See Mark 9:23; 10:27; Hebrews 11:1; Revelation 21:5.

toward the unloved, we squeeze tightly shut; our mouths, with which you would proclaim release, we open to declare we won't get involved.

Convict us, Lord! Teach us that the world is not ours for us to conquer, but yours for us to tend! Convince us that we are not to retreat from the world, but return to it, filled with your compassion. Empower us, Lord! As we commit ourselves to you in this place, remind us that our commitment is meaningless if we do not exercise it in other places. As we dedicate ourselves to you in this hour, remind us that our dedication is unacceptable if we do not express it in other hours. Let your will be our will; your kingdom, our kingdom; your power, our power; and your glory, our glory—on earth as it is in heaven, forever and ever!

❧ *Sunday Between July 31 and August 6.* O Lord of the Good Harvest, receive the prayer of those who plow fields and scatter seed upon the earth, those who build barns and fill them with the fruit of their labors. We come before you humbly, asking that you enter our barns and inspect our crops. Look within us and judge whether we are rich toward you or for ourselves. Where we are found wanting, convict us, and create in us a new heart.

We confess, O Lord, that we often scatter bad seed, and the world reaps the evil we sow. We sow the seeds of anger. Sometimes the anger is ours, and we let it explode into harm—or we bury it, and allow it to fester. Sometimes we arouse anger in others, and we refuse to see it—or seeing, we refuse to address it. Forgive us, O God, when we scatter seeds of anger.

We also plant seeds of malice. We act spitefully, we act vindictively; we inflict abuse upon others, we incite violence against body and spirit. Forgive us, O God, when we scatter seeds of malice.

We acknowledge too that we spread seeds of deception. Our words cannot be trusted, our works cannot be taken at face value. We consider sincerity a sign of naiveté; we regard integrity as old-fashioned. Forgive us, O God, when we scatter seeds of deception.

Our barns are full, O Lord, but they are bursting with bitter fruits. Where we keep anger, you would have stored compassion; where we keep malice, you would have stored love; where we keep deception, you would have stored truth. Compassion, love, truth: These and more you would have us sow and reap, increase and multiply, that all might eat and be filled, drink and be satisfied, make merry and be thankful, being rich toward you, the Provider of Life.

Destroy the bad seed within us, Lord. Burn our dross with the purifying fire, and make room for new seeds, new works, new harvests. Help us to plant your seeds and tend your fields, and the mustard trees of your realm will flourish, fed by the waters of justice rolling down your holy mountain.

✹ *Sunday Between August 7 and August 13.*   O God, who confronts us with hopeful tomorrows, despite our rebellious yesterdays, we approach you in gratitude. We put ourselves in your hands, though our sins be like scarlet, assured that you can take all that is wrong with us and make it right, that you can take all that is good about us and make it better.

We do not sing about "amazing grace" simply because a hymn writer has composed the lines. We sing about it because your grace at work in our life has never ceased to amaze us. We marvel at its power to transplant and to transform. Your grace turned Abraham and Sarah from comfortable residents of a reputable city into tent-dwelling but happy nomads; your grace turned Moses from a stammering youth into an eloquent liberator; your grace turned Ruth from an obscure widow into a determined heroine; your grace turned Isaiah from a preacher of judgment into a proclaimer of forgiveness; your grace turned Mary from a scorned refugee into a keeper of divine secrets; your grace turned Saul, a fierce persecutor of Christians, into Paul, a forceful proclaimer of Christian faith.

Your grace at work in human life is no less amazing today. "The old, old story" can be repeated, if only we can transcend our past: a past when we were less circumspect about the places we frequented; less careful about the power we wielded; less scrupulous about the money we spent; less concerned about the practices we encouraged. O Lord, release us from our past, that we might experience the freedom for which Christ set us free, and serve one another in love.

We do not pray for ourselves alone. We pray for all whose tomorrows are overcast with the shadows of their yesterdays. Blot out their painful memories, and deliver us from the temptation to rekindle their pain. Let us remember that you do not appoint us either as judges over them or as keepers of their conscience. You *do* appoint us to open the door when they knock, that they might come in and sup with you, and you with them.

We thank you, dear Lord, that your amazing grace still abounds, and that, just as you made our ancestors its channel for us, you make us its channel for others. If there be in us any obstacle to its flow, we pray that you will not let it remain. Remove it far from us, so that in days to come, when your people sing "Amazing Grace," they will praise you— not as the God of the past but as the God of the present; not as the God who was but as the God who *is*—is now, and evermore shall be.

❈ *Sunday Between August 14 and August 20.* O God of endless surprises, who chastens us when we look for comfort and comforts us when we look for chastening, who challenges us when we expect to be praised and praises us when we expect to be challenged, you are the Lord our God, the one before whom we bow in fear and trembling, in adoration and praise. Sometimes we would prefer that you be a little more predictable and not quite so full of surprises! If only your ways were not so different from ours and your thoughts so much higher than ours! Then we could come before you in confidence and pride. But we would not know who should be praying to whom. So we thank you, dear Lord, for your frequent reminders of the distance between you and ourselves.

We wish we could do without these reminders, but daily we prove our need for them. We sound warnings of your judgment, and when it does not strike, we doubt not our knowledge, but your power. We call for the destruction of our enemies, and when they are not destroyed, we question not our righteousness, but your justice. We seek places of honor, and when others obtain them, we indict not our ambition, but your faithfulness. We pray for peace with justice, and when we must settle for injustice without peace, we question not our passion, but your commitment. Not only do we hold you responsible for the wrongs we do. We also hold you responsible for the wrongs *we* could *undo*—if only instead of looking up for the problem, we would look within; if only instead of looking within for the solution, we would look up.

Forgive us, O God, for the shameful way we exonerate ourselves at your expense. We blame you for things for which we are responsible, and we praise ourselves for things for which you are responsible. We are quick to indict those who frustrate our quest for fulfillment, and slow to credit those who advance it. Yet a cloud of your witnesses surrounds us. They are those who look not to Washington or Wall Street for guidance, but to the prophets and apostles; who slay the dragon of personal greed on the altar of human service; who risk failure for the sake of honesty rather than seek advantage through dishonesty; who measure success not by the speed with which they move up but by the grace with which they reach out. If we have yet to catch a glimpse of these people, open our eyes, dear Lord. Forgive us for allowing our sight to become so distorted that we no longer can separate the wheat from the chaff.

Open our eyes, O Lord, that we might behold among us those who incarnate the spirit of the one who incarnated your spirit. Open our imaginations, that we might behold within us another candidate for the incarnation of that same spirit. And open our hearts, that we might behold around us still others who are anxious to receive your grace. They are ready and waiting. Help us, dear Lord, to make sure they must wait no longer.

❧ *Sunday Between August 21 and August 27.*　O gracious God, to whose greatness our worship adds nothing, but without whose worship we diminish everything, we lift our hearts and voices in gratitude for the opportunity of worship; for this place in which to render worship; and for the church of Jesus Christ, whose spirit always informs our worship—and sometimes inspires us to *reform* our worship.

We are grateful for your prophets, who shine the light of your judgment into the dark corners of our lives. At the time, we may not know that it costs them as much pain to expose us as it costs us to be exposed. But the fact of their pain dawns upon us, once we heed their rebuke and see that their joy is as great as ours. O God, we thank you for these truth-sayers, without whom we truth-seekers might substitute our camaraderie with one another for communion with you. If we are troubled by the presence of your prophets, let us ask ourselves if we have not become too comfortable in *your* presence. Help us to realize that the only thing we need fear from the prophets is their absence or, worse, a church in which they are silenced.

We confess, O Lord, that this lesson is not an easy one. Often, when persons speak to us in your name, we listen not to those who confront us with your judgment, but to those who console us with your favor; not to those who highlight our responsibilities, but to those who keynote our privileges; not to those who stress our equality with others, but to those who emphasize our superiority. We wish we could blame your misguided prophets for our betrayal of you, but we know our deceitful hearts give wings to deceitful tongues.

Forgive us, dear God, for our selfishness of heart: the selfishness that makes us insensitive to your word, indifferent to your messengers, and unfaithful to your mission. Renew our appreciation for the church as the body of Christ, and for ourselves as its members, open to your guidance and committed to your service. As Christ has opened the door of your kingdom to all your children, let us open the doors of his church to all your children, that his unanswered prayer that we become one—even as you and he are one—might be answered in our lifetime.

O God, even as we lament the divisions that afflict your church, let us labor to heal the divisions that plague your world. Let not the Christians in lands of persecution and poverty be forgotten in lands of peace and plenty. Give to your church a mind quick to sense the needs of all its members; a heart able to feel their pain; and a hand ready to offer the help for which they long. Make the church, like the Christ to whom it bears witness, a beacon for all humanity.

❦ *Sunday Between August 28 and September 3.*   O Lord of love, who instructs us in all the ways we can be taught, and who seeks us in all the ways we can be found, you are our Teacher, without whose instruction we would be constantly confused; and our Guide, without whose companionship we would daily go astray. We thank you for your generosity, for your readiness so freely and fully to teach us and to lead us.

We thank you, too, that you were equally generous to our ancestors, while always careful to adapt your presence to their need, just as you do to ours. Not only did you give them the law for shaping their life, but you gave them your love for reshaping their law. Let us not mistake your guidance and instruction of them for your guidance and instruction of us. But let us deal justly and gently with our ancestors, learning from their mistakes and profiting from their insights.

We must confess, O God, that we have been slow to do so. While our ancestors asserted the power of grace to beget goodness, we withhold the offer of grace until we behold the evidence of goodness. While they encouraged hospitality to strangers, we act as strangers even toward our neighbors. While they remembered those in prison as if imprisoned with them, we shun prisoners as if they were not human beings. While they steeled themselves against love of money, we pursue riches as if they were all that mattered. While they felt the pain of injustice as if its victims, we leave the campaign for justice to others.

O God, help us to realize that if we do not walk in your ways, it is not always because our ancestors have neglected to teach your word. As often as not, it is because we have ignored their wise counsel and good example. The fault lies not with previous generations, but with ours. Those in need of forgiveness are neither the people who came before us nor the people who live around us, but ourselves.

Forgive us, dear God, for denying our responsibility for the world in which we dwell. Grant us the grace neither to blame our ancestors for our mistakes nor to rob our descendants of their birthright. Help us to bequeath to them a world that will respect their dignity and honor their dreams—a world that will nurture body, mind, and spirit, with privilege for all and prejudice for none.

O Lord, bless the ties that bind us to those who have gone before and to those who shall come after. We pray for wisdom, lest we become so obsessed with yesterday's mistakes that we hesitate to seize today's opportunities; and we pray for courage, lest we become so despondent over our failure to make the world perfect that we stop trying to make it better. Help us to demand of ourselves neither more nor less than we demand of our ancestors and descendants. Let us acknowledge the members of all generations as our sisters and brothers in your family, that we might honor you by honoring them.

❀ *Sunday Between September 4 and September 10.*

O Christ, revealer of God to us and of us to God, you are unlike any-thing, unlike any*one* we have ever known, eternally faithful to God and infinitely faithful to God's people. Yet you risk everything, entrusting us with the work of your holy realm, just as God has entrusted us with the stewardship of the natural world. You ask that we be filled with your spirit, that we become like you—you, whose consolations cheer our souls when the cares of our hearts are too many; you, whose dreams inspire our souls when the burdens on our hearts are too heavy; you, whose words enlighten our souls when the eyes of our hearts are too blind; you, whose deeds humble our souls when the intentions of our hearts are too proud. How you honor us, Lord! And how we would honor you!

How gracious you are! Though you have the authority and the power simply to command us to do whatever you need us to do, yet for love's sake, you *appeal* to us, that we might *choose* to do good, freely and not by compulsion. How gracious you are, that you do not just overwhelm us with what you require—that instead, you invite us to unite our will with yours! How you honor us, Lord! And how we would honor you!

Yet we are tempted to keep you at a safe distance, so that when you call, we can pretend not to hear; when you point to where we are needed, we can seem preoccupied; when you grip our arm, we can pull away. As if you might tire of troubling us with tasks we don't want, and turn to someone else for help—someone with more time, more money, more power, more personality, more talent, more status, more reason, more *something!* We *do* admire what you desire, Lord, but even we know that admiration is not devotion. Devotion is far more costly, and we are not sure we really want to pay that cost. Devotion is the bearing of a cross, and we are not sure we really want to carry that cross.

O Christ, forgive us for seeking far more from you than we are willing to give in return—not only to you, but to all those to whom you would have us give. Fill our hearts with an unwavering resolve and an unceasing love. Help us to be unlike anyone we have ever known—anyone except you; make us eternally faithful to you and infinitely faithful to your people. Help us to risk everything as we labor in your vineyard and care for the world. Refresh us with your spirit, that we might cheer our neighbors when the cares of their hearts are too many; inspire them when the burdens on their hearts are too heavy; enlighten them when the eyes of their hearts are too blind; and humble them when the intentions of their hearts are too proud.

We pray these things out of the greatness and the smallness of our faith—a faith given not to this world, but to the world that is to come.

❦ *Sunday Between September 11 and September 17.*

O Lord, the mountains tremble and the clouds pour forth rain; the skies thunder, and lightning flashes on every side. Your voice is in the whirlwind, and your path is through the waters that roar and foam—yours is a broad and mighty road, yet your footprints are unseen! You come and go, and though you never really leave us, you never really show yourself, either. Miracles, wonders, signs: These are small things to which we cling, as if they somehow document your faithfulness. We cling to them steadfastly, although time and again you warn us not to erect our house of faith upon them, lest it collapse in a storm like a house built upon sand.[45]

---

45. Inspired by Psalm 46:3; Matthew 7:24-27.

Temptation is powerful, Lord. We ignore your warning. We shore up our faith by construing our success as proof of your faithfulness: We interpret our prosperity as your blessing, our good fortune as your favor, a turn of luck as your sign of approval, a lack of resistance as your sanction. We are so intent upon earning your love for ourselves that our neighbors are soon left unnoticed, unseen, unheard, misunderstood, mistreated.

So now you have a quarrel with us, Lord. And we are surprised, but without cause. You have watched in open-mouthed astonishment as we turned away from one another, thinking that we were turning toward you. You have watched as faithfulness has faded from the land, as kindness fell victim to neglect, as trust was strained and broken. You have watched us walk in and out of church, offering you tithes while withholding our lives, and you have been amazed that we did not hear the grieving of creation. We did not pay attention to her sorrow; her beasts in the field, her birds in the air, her fish in the sea—they vanished. The fruits of the trees rotted, the crops in the fields were choked by weeds. Our toil turned empty, our art became a lament, our eyes scrutinized every person we met, and we wondered: Is he my enemy? Is she my competition? In all the land no one asks: Isn't he my brother? Isn't she my sister? Isn't that little one my child? Isn't that elder one my parent?

Help us, Lord! Forgive us, for we have sinned! You desire us to know you; we have tried to *win* you. You desire love; we have given liturgy. You desire justice; we have sung a song. You desire righteousness; we have planned solemn assemblies.[46]

O God, show us your face! Show us a face whose eyes dream of justice, that the same dream might burn in our eyes. Show us a face whose mouth proclaims the love of kindness, that the same proclamation might issue from our mouths.[47] What do you require of us but to walk humbly with you and our neighbors? Revive us! Raise us up! Give us strength! For there is so much that must be done, and so much that must be undone.

O Lord, let the mountains tremble, and we shall embrace those who tremble with them. Let the clouds pour forth their rain, and we shall carry the water to the thirsty. Let the skies thunder, and we shall open

---

46. Inspired by Amos 5:21-24.
47. Inspired by Micah 6:8.

the ears of the deaf. Let lightning flash on every side, and we shall heal the eyes of the blind. Miracles, wonders, signs: These are the things that we shall do for your children out of the abundance of faithfulness. We shall cling steadfastly—not to what we *do,* but to who our neighbors are, and to who we are when we are with them. Help us to build our house upon love, for we know that a house built upon love will stand firm in the fullness of your presence, even as a house built upon rock.[48]

❧ *Sunday Between September 18 and September 24.*

O Lord, our Lord, you are the salve of the soul: Hear our supplications! The soul of our world is weary, needing your balm. Its past is a burden on our shoulders; its present is a stumbling block before our feet; its tomorrow is lost in a vast maze, for which we can find no map. Everything is shifting, changing so fast that the very earth trembles. We lose our footing and fall, only to be dragged along the ground by some unseen hand that will not let us go. We are frightened, Lord. Sometimes we feel weak and helpless; sometimes we feel angry and powerless. So we have returned to you, the Faithful One, our Help in time of trouble. We return to you and ask for courage. We return to you and ask for wisdom.

O Lord, our Lord, you are the prophecy of the spirit: Hear our prayers! The spirit of our world is torn, needing your voice. Its lands are rent by war and wrong; its peoples are divided by color and creed and class and culture; its unity is ripped into a million shreds, and we can find no pattern by which to mend. Everything is straining, pulling apart so hard that the very earth groans. We yearn for a word, Lord. Sometimes we feel ignorant and foolish; sometimes we feel overwhelmed and defenseless. So we have returned to you, the Faithful One, our Voice in time of trouble. We return to you and ask for judgment. We return to you and ask for clarity.

O Lord, our Lord, you are the inner movings of the heart: Hear our intercessions! The heart of our world is indifferent, needing your stimulation. Its eyes refuse to look upon the suffering; its ears refuse to listen to the abused; its lips refuse to speak out for the oppressed. Everything is numb, paralyzed so deeply that the very earth sleeps. Stir us awake, Lord. Sometimes we feel dead and listless; sometimes we feel cut off

---

48. Inspired by Matthew 7:24-27.

and hopeless. So we have returned to you, the Faithful One, our Inspiration in time of trouble. We return to you and ask for revival. We return to you and ask for resurrection.

O Lord, our Lord, you are the thoughts of the mind: Hear our thanksgivings! The mind of our world is confused, needing your counsel, and we trust that you will grant understanding. If its intentions are not honorable; if its ambitions are not just; if its aspirations are not fair; if everything is muddled, so clouded that the very earth doubts its turning on its axis, we believe that you will make things plain. If we feel bewildered and aimless; if we feel defeated and hapless, you will give direction. For this we have returned to you, the Faithful One, our Hope in time of trouble. We have returned to ask for your salvation; we have returned to ask for your presence; and we know that we shall receive.

❧ *Sunday Between September 25 and October 1.*　O God, you cross back and forth across the earth to recover all who are lost in oppression and sorrow. And you pour contempt upon the tormentors of their bodies and souls, causing them to wander in trackless wastes until they perceive the error of their ways. We praise you for raising up those who are needy and afflicted and for bringing low those who magnify their need and affliction. We praise you with hopeful and with penitent hearts, for we have been both the persecuted you save and the persecutors you scorn.

You know even better than we, O Lord, that we have lived on both sides of the great and growing chasm that separates those who have enough from those who do not—that deep and deepening gulf between those who feast sumptuously every day and those who, like Lazarus, lie outside the gate, fed only with scraps from the others' table. We confess that when we hear the parable of the rich person and Lazarus, we identify with the suffering one, wishing we could receive more compassion and be relieved of our pain, in this life as in the next. We *have* experienced great pain, Lord, and we are grateful that you are willing to enter our lives to transform that pain; that you reach to embrace us with the caring arms of friends and family, or perhaps even a stranger; that you seek to save us by whatever means your spirit can inspire. You do, indeed, come to us in the desert.

But, Lord, too often we aspire to be the wealthy. We desire to have more than we have, even when more would be too much. Our desire grows like an insatiable appetite and leads us into temptation. Our feet become ensnared in traps we set for others, or in traps we did not mean to set at all. Our senseless ambitions plunge even innocent people into pain and ruin. Watching, scheming, pinching, planning, we eventually cannot stand the misery, and we seek some way to escape it.

Great and saving God, convict us: Show us how grievous a sin it is to set our hopes on uncertain riches. Teach us to rest our lives on you, who so richly provides for us, and who would have us so faithfully provide for others. Help us to do good, to become rich in the compassion of liberal hearts and generous hands. We are your workers; direct us in our labor. Show us how to close the chasm that cuts any one of us off from the rest of us, that every rich one might join hands with every Lazarus, that all of us might take hold of the life that is life indeed.

❧ *Sunday Between October 2 and October 8.* O Christ, who sensed the danger of depending upon others but did not hesitate to brave that danger; who knew the pain of rebuking friends but did not hesitate to risk that pain; who counted the cost of discipleship but did not hesitate to pay that cost: we adore you. You are our Lord, before whom we bow in awe and gratitude, and our Teacher, to whom we turn in need and expectation. As you have taught us the meaning of lordship, teach us the meaning of discipleship; teach us what it means to be members not simply of the church but of your body.

This is not the first time we have approached you as disciples seeking guidance. We have approached you many times, and each time you heeded our request. But we did not always heed your counsel. You urged us to honor those who serve God by sharing their faith, but we coveted the honor for ourselves. You reminded us to warn against the consequences of evil deeds, but we feared the scorn of evildoers. You exhorted us to treat all persons alike, in the world as in the church, but we played favorites in the church as in the world. You have not failed us, Lord; we have failed you.

So we come to you, asking for another chance—not a second chance but a third or fourth or fifth chance. We ask for the grace to hear and to heed your voice; for the fortitude to confront and to correct our friends; for the determination to respect and to rely on others; and for the courage to count and to pay the cost of discipleship. We are not ignorant of the demands of discipleship, but we have not done justice by our knowledge. Help us, O Christ, to do as well as we know and, better yet, to do the greater works you promised we would do.

We thank you, dear Lord, for greeting us as brothers and sisters; for making us disciples to one another, that we might minister to one another in your spirit. Grant us the grace to be open to one another, so that when one rejoices we all rejoice, and when one suffers we all suffer. As the world learned of your lordship by your love for us, let the world learn of our discipleship by our love for one another. Rekindle within us the gift of God; stir within us the spirit of power! Bless us, and in faith and love we will proclaim your truth.

❧ *Sunday Between October 9 and October 15.* O Christ of the transforming look, who sees in us what others overlook and overlooks in us what others see, we thank you for your sight, the source of our hope and the goal of our striving.

Once, upon discovering that we were blind followers of the blind, we prayed for *our* sight. But no longer. Now we pray for *your* sight, so that when we look at God, we will see not an angry judge but a gracious parent; when we look at our neighbors, we will see not objects for exploitation but partners in creation; when we look at ourselves, we will see neither a tyrant towering over others nor a servant cowering before others, but a disciple ministering unto others.

O Lord, as you grant us your sight, deliver us from *our* sight, which has often been a source of frustration and distortion. In our sight God has been not the dispenser of grace but the distributor of justice; our neighbors, not those to whom we could give help but those from whom we could receive help; and ourselves, not followers of your way but captives of our own. In our sight disciples have been not reformers of hearts but performers of rites. In our sight sinners have been not persons unto whom we should draw near but nobodies from whom we should steer clear. In our sight foreigners have been not a reason for celebrating the wideness of God's love but a cause for lamenting the loss of our privilege. Too long, O Lord, we have looked at the world through our own eyes, and the world has suffered the consequences of our impaired vision.

Help us, O Christ, to look at the teachings and traditions of our religion through your eyes. Should our religion claim that we believers deserve better than others, that we should be granted the friendship of the powerful and spared the company of the marginal, let us recognize that our inherited beliefs have distorted your incarnate faith. When this happens, give us the grace to acknowledge the conflict and the courage to resolve it in the spirit with which you set your face toward Jerusalem.[49] As we examine the church, endow us with the clarity of your vision, lest the gap between your church and our church grow ever wider and deeper.

We pray also, O Christ, for the gift of your sight as we examine the world. Let us behold you, enthroned in majesty at the right hand of God, staring the powers of this world in the face, refusing to render unto them what belongs to God. Let us never forget that it was for the reconciliation of the world unto God that you laid down your life. Let our eyes be anointed with your healing touch, that as we encounter the world, we might continue your work of reconciliation.

❦ *Sunday Between October 16 and October 22.*   O God of compassionate prophets, hear us now, though we have been neither compassionate nor prophetic. We have witnessed the workings of your word through the Moseses and the Miriams, through the Daniels and the Deborahs—through those who lived long before us and through those who live among us. You have caused their eyes to see wrongs and to look upon troubles. Their souls have watched until your fire was kindled within them, and they began to rage against the destruction and violence being wrought, at the contention and strife being waged. Your prophets see, and seethe, and finally speak—but do we hear? Have we faith?

How fearful we are, Lord, of our world as it is; but how much more fearful of what it might take to make it different! When your prophets counsel peace, we are afraid to lay down our arms. So we remind the prophets that Christ said, "You have heard that you shall love your neighbor and hate your enemy," forgetting that in the next moment, he declared, "I say love your enemies and pray for those who persecute you." When your prophets denounce poverty, we are afraid to give up our wealth. So we remind the prophets that Christ said, "You will always have the poor with you," forgetting that in the next breath, he declared, "Do good to them." When your prophets decry prejudice, we are afraid to share our status. So we remind the prophets that Christ said, "I was sent only to the house of Israel; I will not throw the children's bread to the dogs," forgetting that in the next moment, he declared, "O Canaanite woman, great is your faith! Be it done as you

---

49. See Luke 9:51.

desire!" When your prophets attack false piety, we are afraid to confess our pride. So we remind the prophets that Christ said, "This people honors me with their lips," forgetting that in the next breath, he declared, "But their heart is far from me; they leave the commandment of God and hold fast to their own traditions." [50]

Again and again, O God, you have raised up your prophets; again and again you have made their lips burn—but we have been more willing to rid ourselves of them than to risk ourselves for you. So if you would change our world, you will need to change *us!* Send your spirit upon *us;* make *our* souls burn; make *us* your messengers, that we might declare an end to the destruction and violence and contention and strife of which we once were the agents.

Change us, Lord; make us your people: a people equipped not merely for work, but for *good* work; a people prepared not merely for life, but for *faithful* life; a people united not merely in spirit, but in a *gracious* spirit; a people inspired not merely by love, but by an *inexhaustible, unquenchable* love. Change us, and in your name we shall curse enmity, and war shall be no more; we shall curse poverty, and want shall be no more; we shall curse prejudice, and bigotry shall be no more; we shall curse false piety, and hypocrisy shall be no more. Change us; make us whole, and when your word is spoken, when Christ is come among us, there will, indeed, be found a people of faith on earth.

❦ *Sunday Between October 23 and October 29.*　O Christ our Lord, support of the righteous and troubler of the self-righteous, help of the faithful and hope of the faithless, you are our refuge and strength, a very present help in trouble. Not only are you there just *when* we need you most. You are there just *as* we need you most: to confront us when we need to be confronted; to comfort us when we need to be comforted; to correct us when we need to be corrected; to commend us when we need to be commended. You are the answer— not only to our prayer but to our need. So we thank you for your readiness to honor us with your presence and for your determination to transform us *by* your presence.

From the dawn of history until the present, you have been with us, leading us away from temptation into the paths of righteousness. You

---

50. See Matthew 5:43-44; Mark 14:7; Matthew 15:26-28; Mark 7:6-7.

endowed us with all the gifts necessary to discern your presence among us. You gave us a heart for understanding your motives, a mind for deciphering your will, eyes for discovering your purpose, ears for hearing your summons, and hands and feet for performing your commands. Yet we have let these gifts lie dormant. And now we and our world are in trouble—not because of your absence but because of our insensitivity to your presence.

You have been present to instruct us in the ways of peace with justice. You tried to teach us the wisdom of turning swords into plowshares, but we have turned them into tanks and missiles. You tried to teach us the wisdom of preventing conflict by eliminating hunger, but we have played politics and ignored poverty. You tried to teach us the wisdom of using persuasion rather than coercion, but we have practiced intimidation. With shame we confess, O Lord, that we could have learned a great deal more from our history, if only we had acknowledged your presence and heeded your instruction. We must also confess that we have not profited as we should from your presence in the lives of your faithful ones. In them you gave us clues to your will, but we have preferred to follow our own.

Forgive us, O Christ, for having been such inept students of history and of humanity. Enable us to learn from experience—our own as well as the experience of others; help us to profit from mistakes—the mistakes of others as well as our own. Let us feel your presence at work in others for our sake; let others feel your presence at work in us for their sake.

❦ *Sunday Between October 30 and November 5.*

O Spirit, you are the voice that will never fail to sing, though all the world be silent; you are the foot that will never fail to dance, though all the world be still. You are the eye that will never fail to watch, though all the world be sleeping; you are the mind that will never fail to reason, though all the world be senseless. You are the hand that will never fail to open, though all the world be selfish; you are the heart that will never fail to feel, though all the world be numb.

Thank you, Spirit, for abiding in our midst, for moving us when we do not want to move and for slowing us down when we do not want to stop. Thank you for moving in ways that, though mysterious, do not frighten us away. We are a people often made small by the greatness of our fear. We shrink from conflict when conflict cries out for resolution.

We flee from truth when truth demands expression. We run from change when change must come: change that will require us to be no longer who we have been, to do no longer as we have done, to say no longer what we have said, to believe no longer as we have believed.

O Comforter, remain among us, and we will rise above our fear. Instead of shrinking from conflict, we will join it until it is justly resolved. Instead of fleeing from truth, we will pursue it until it is freely expressed. Instead of running from change, we will weigh it until it is fairly judged.

O Spirit, abide among us, and we will rise above all fear. We will become your voice, and though all else be silent, we will never cease to sing your song. We will become your feet, and though all else be still, we will never cease to dance your dance. We will become your eyes, and though all else be sleeping, we will never cease to keep your watch. We will become your mind, and though all else be senseless, we will never cease to seek your will. We will become your hands, and though all else be selfish, we will never cease to share your riches. We will become your heart, and though all else be numb, we will never fail to love your world.

❧ *Sunday Between November 6 and November 12.*
O God of parables and riddles, how you tantalize our minds by your glory! We marvel at your universe, stretching beyond the reach of any human eye or telescope; we behold infinity in a blade of grass and eternity in a drop of water. The vision of life is too great—it blinds us; we raise our hands, we turn our heads from the brilliant light. Relieve the burning magnificence of your presence, Lord; do you not know that we are only human?

O God of mysteries and secrets, how you tempt us by your love! We wonder at your faithfulness, stretching beyond the reach of any human heart or promise; we feel boundless compassion at the touch of your hand and endless forgiveness at the sound of your voice. The experience of your love is too much—it dazes us; we fall on our knees, we reach for you in the trembling air. Relieve the overwhelming fullness of your presence, Lord; do you not know that we are only human?

O, but you do know! You have endured long centuries of our sinful ways, and your ears have grown heavy from our monotonous defense: "We are only human, Lord!" we have said. "You expect too much!" Your heart has groaned as we have wrestled with your angels, crying,

"How can we mortals be righteous before God? How can we human beings be pure before our Maker? How can the Lord trust us, who dwell in houses of clay, who are crushed before the moth? How can the Holy One have faith in us, who drink iniquity like water?"[51] Your heart has broken as we have contended with your heavens, shouting, *"You do not need us!* How can a human be profitable to a god? Surely in your power you require no help!"[52]

Yes, Lord; you know well that we are only mortal, for only we have been so proud as to declare our utter independence from you in one breath and our utter dependence upon you in the next. And only we, among all your creatures, have dared to question your goodness in creating us and our dignity in *being* us; we have equated our existence with that of the miserable worm,[53] as if you had not also made the worm and provided for its place!

O God, remind us that being "only human" is meant not to be a cause for shame, but celebration. We are yours—your children, your people; and like our sister, the caterpillar,[54] we are born to be reborn, to awaken from sleep to the spirit, and to put on the colorful clothes of your glory and love.

Convince us, Lord, of the truth of your parables and riddles; persuade us of the revelation of your mysteries and secrets. For all that is revealed is One: All that is revealed is You, who are the union of Life and Love. Let us stop degrading our humanity by appealing to our weakness. We are children of deity, humanity born of heaven. To abase ourselves is to blaspheme you. To separate ourselves from you is to commit sacrilege against you. Let the words of our lips increase the word of your mouth; let the works of our lives magnify the work of your hand!

❧ *Sunday Between November 13 and November 19.*

O God of heaven and earth, your prophets and apostles teach us to anticipate "the day of the Lord"—a time when wrong will be righted and the righteous honored, when violence will be rejected and the peacemakers acclaimed, when injustice will be outlawed and the just

---

51. See Job 4:17-20; 15:16.
52. Inspired by Job 22:2.
53. See Psalm 22:6.
54. Inspired by Job 17:14.

praised, when guilt will be acknowledged and the innocent acquitted. We give thanks that you are our God, for only a God like you can breathe hope into our life and grant meaning to our existence.

Enable us, O Lord, when we think of your day, to remember the character of the One whose day it is. Help us to put the emphasis where it belongs: not on the fact you *will be* our Judge but on the fact you *are* our Judge; not on your power to wound us then but on our power to wound you now. Let us not forget that the Lord whom we shall meet on your day is no other than the One we have met in Jesus Christ our Lord, in whom you have warned us of the evils you deplore and alerted us to the virtues you uphold.

O God, you warn us not to think more highly of ourselves than we ought, but we honor ourselves before our neighbors. You warn us not to return evil for evil, but we seek an eye for an eye. You warn us that your gospel can turn friends into enemies, but we are anxious if all do not speak well of us. Yes, Lord, you warn us of the evils you deplore, but we do not shun them. Sadder but wiser, we pray for another chance.

We also fail to embrace the virtues to which you alert us. You appeal to us to grant justice to the weak, but we continue to concede privilege to the strong. You appeal to us to show partiality to the orphan, but we question our responsibility to atone for inequity. You appeal to us to maintain the rights of the afflicted, but we regard their defense as a charity case. You appeal to us to rescue the needy, but we stand idly by while their numbers multiply. Yes, Lord, you call us to the virtues you uphold, but we do not embrace them. Sadder but wiser, we pray for another chance.

Forgive us, O God, for our insensitivity to your warnings and appeals and, even more, to the agony of those in whose behalf you utter them. Bestow on us the gifts of your Holy Spirit, that we might become agents of your will, taking your warnings to heart and heeding your appeals. As we go forth in your name, grant us the faith that moves people, the hope that builds community, and the love that creates family.

🍁 *Last Sunday After Pentecost.*   O Maker of covenants and Keeper of promises, you are the cornerstone of our faith and the foundation of our hope!

You are the Rock, opening yourself so that water might flow for those wandering in the wilderness;

You are the Rock, raising yourself up amid desert wastes to offer shade in a weary land;

You are the Rock, making yourself level when the way is rough, that the foot of the traveler might be secure;

You are the Rock, speaking when no other voice is heard and hearing when no other ear is bent; [55]

You are the Rock, in which there is no unrighteousness, in which there is great refuge; [56]

You are the Rock, from which the death-tomb is hewn, and you are the stone, rolling away from its door;

You are the Rock, from which your people are fashioned, and on which our house and your kingdom stand! [57]

Yes, Lord, you are our Rock: the cornerstone of our faith and the foundation of our hope. Therefore, we pray, strengthen us with all power, according to your glorious might, that we may be filled with the endurance of your mountains, standing against rain and wind and earthquake and fire. Strengthen us, that we may be filled with the patience of your rivers, flowing against forces intent on slowing them down or damming them up. Strengthen us, that we may be filled with the joy of your harvest, singing as the fields are crowned with bounty and the valleys are clothed with grain. [58]

O God, as in Christ all your fullness was pleased to dwell, so make us fit vessels for your indwelling spirit. As through Christ you sought to reconcile all things, so make us instruments of your reconciliation. And as by Christ you worked to establish peace, so make us agents of your peacemaking.

You are our salvation, Lord. Standing on any other ground, we can do nothing; standing on you, we can do everything. [59] Sinking in sand, all is impossible; building on rock, all things are possible. [60] In the name of all that can be done, in the spirit of all that is possible, we commit ourselves to your cause, our Strength and our Redeemer!

---

55. Inspired by Exodus 17:6-7; Psalm 95:1; Isaiah 32:2; Psalm 40:2; II Samuel 23:3; Psalm 28:1.
56. See Psalm 92:15; II Samuel 22:2.
57. Inspired by Luke 23:53; 24:2; Isaiah 51:1; Matthew 7:24; 16:8.
58. See Psalm 65:11-13.
59. See Philippians 4:13.
60. Inspired by Matthew 19:26; 7:24-27.

Dear God,

Each day is an occasion for giving thanks for life and the range of colors through which it passes. But on this day, O God, we pause to thank you for particular lives. We thank you for the people whose death brought to our souls the dark night of sorrow and whose living memory now brings us the golden light of day. Not all of them were saints, but each of them possessed something worth remembering, something loved, something sacred, something honorable, something good. For the life of each of these persons, and for the lives of all those who have no one to remember their names, we give you thanks.

We thank you, O God, for holding in your care those you sent ahead of us. They prepared a road, marking its pitfalls, digging wells for our thirst, building shelters for our rest. Not always did they know who would follow them, but they pressed on. Sometimes they stumbled, many times they were injured, but on they went, carrying a spark of the divine.

Now we journey that road, which is different yet the same. Constantly we are reminded of their presence—things we see and hear, feel and do are so very familiar, so reminiscent of those gone before. Yet we are beyond them.

To realize that we are beyond them can be frightening. Now that *we* are preparing the way for those to come, we are awed by the responsibility. For should we fail in these preparations, we will dishonor past generations, disinherit future generations, and discredit our God.

Let us not forget these faceless travelers who shall come after us. Let us be known to them, not by the broken world they inherit, but in the breaking of the bread of life. Guide our preparations with your Spirit. Help us to be remembered for the good fruits of our labor! *Amen.*

Index of Key Words and Themes

Index of Key Words and Themes